ZETTERBERG, HANS LENNART
ON THEORY AND VERIFICATION IN

KU-762-613

HM24.Z61/

University of Liverpool

Withdrawn from stock

# ON THEORY AND VERIFICATION
## IN SOCIOLOGY

# ON THEORY AND VERIFICATION

# IN SOCIOLOGY

*by*

HANS L. ZETTERBERG

*A Much Revised Edition*

THE BEDMINSTER PRESS

1963

Copyright © 1954, Almquist & Wiksell

Copyright © 1963, The Bedminster Press

Totowa, New Jersey


Manufactured in the United States of America


Library of Congress Catalogue Card Number 63-13894

*Readers of this book are invited to send name and address
to* THE BEDMINSTER PRESS, *Vreeland Avenue, Totowa,
New Jersey, U.S.A., to receive announcements and literature
about other books in the social sciences published by*
THE BEDMINSTER PRESS.

R7143

# TABLE OF CONTENTS

*"We may have many concepts but few confirmed theories; many points of view, but few theorems; many 'approaches' but few arrivals. Perhaps a shift in emphasis would be all to the good."*

Robert K. Merton

## PREFACE TO THE SECOND EDITION

More than half of the material in this little book is new in the sense that it was not included in its first edition. Deletions from the first edition are equally extensive; also, everything relating to definitions, taxonomy, and descriptive studies has been reserved for a later, separate treatment.

In making these revisions I have benefited greatly from comments on the first edition. I would like to thank particularly Professors B. Andersson, G. Boalt, E. Dahlström, T. Hopkins, G. Karlsson, and P. F. Lazarsfeld for their helpful reviews. Parts of the material added to this edition have appeared in German, Italian, and Polish.[1] I am especially grateful for the detailed comments on the German version given by Professors P. F. Lazarsfeld and H. Wold.

It is a coincidence that looks like a forethought that I was in Sweden during both writings of this work. The initial writing was done in 1952 at Professor Segerstedt's Institute at Uppsala University, and the present revision was done in 1963 at Professor Dahlström's Institute at Gothen-

---

[1] The German version contains also some observations on the procedures of taxonomy and descriptive studies which are omitted here. See Hans L. Zetterberg, "Theorie, Forschung und Praxis in der Soziologie," in R. Koenig (ed.), *Handbuch der empirischen Sozialforschung*, vol. I (Stuttgart: Ferdinand Enke Verlag, 1961), pp. 64-104.

burg University. The hospitality and adventurous spirit of reflective inquiry at these Institutes will always remain among my fondest memories. In both places the basic question "How is sociology possible?" was asked in earnest, and in both places I have been pleased to retort that sociology is possible, or at least easier, if it is theoretical. I was rather young and ignorant when I first said it, and I have appreciated this opportunity to say it again, and perhaps a little better.

The intellectual trends of thought and experiences that have shaped my emphasis on theoretical sociology might be briefly sketched. In Sweden my teacher, Torgny T. Segerstedt, like many others in many countries—allowed emphasis on theory to make up for soft methodology. My interest in this issue was aroused when I was called upon to defend this stand in a debate with psychometricians but found nothing written about it. Later I became acquainted with a somewhat parallel American debate of older standing at Columbia University. The issue here was whether sociology would advance more by concentrating on theory—a position taken by Robert K. Merton—or by concentrating on methodology—a position taken by Paul F. Lazarsfeld. I learned much from this discussion, and here again I sided with the theorists. As is evident from my book *Social Theory and Social Practice,* I have even come to trust applied theory as much as applied research.

This bet on theoretical sociology, however, has not emerged because I have rejected the arguments by the methodologists but because I have fully accepted them. As a graduate student at the University of Minnesota, Professors F. Stuart Chapin and Neal E. Gross introduced me to a rigid methodology based on the dictums of logical empiricism, and here I met the strict methodological ideas of George A. Lundberg, not merely as the ideals for research I had known from my first acquaintance with sociology, but as part of ongoing research practice. Using these strict standards, I eventually came to feel—apparently with several colleagues in America and Europe—that not only my own but even the most celebrated research projects in our field left something to be desired from a methodological point of view. And the whole research enterprise conducted in this fashion, which too often rendered trivial conclusions with efforts towards maximum precision, forced me to question sociology as a worthwhile occupation.

In this situation, the call for theory was neither an escape nor just a call for additional requirements to be met. It was simply a call for intellectual salvation. The saving quality of a theory is to *coordinate many methodologically imperfect findings into a rather trustworthy whole,* in the form of a small number of information-packed sentences or equations. Moreover, some of the bits and pieces coordinated into this trustworthy whole can be the challenging insights of the classics of sociology and the celebrated writers of literature: in short, far from trivial propositions.

Contrary to the prevailing emphasis on taxonomical "social theory", it also became clear that only propositional "theoretical sociology" contained such potentialities. This was epitomized in the motto from Robert K. Merton that opened the first edition of this book. The same motto remains for good reasons in the second edition, because the kind of theory it advocates has been drowned by louder taxonomizing voices in the past decade. All signs now are that the next decade will understand it better, and that the theoretical enterprise in sociology will see not only definitions, but more and more propositions, and thus will become theory rather than terminology.

I am enough convinced that this trend represents the future so that the new edition of this small book is conceived, not only as a pamphlet with a polemical cut, but also as a supplementary text which some teachers might find helpful in training future sociologists in courses on sociological research and in courses on sociological theory. As a science, sociology has already bridged the gulf between theory and research; this is true both in principle and in the work of several gifted scholars. The question now is to teach students to run back and forth across this bridge. Our compartmentalized instruction in theory and research might obscure the connection between the two for the students, and we need to establish a better pedagogical tradition at this critical juncture.

I am well aware that this text does not take into account all, or even most, of the niceties elaborated by various philosophies of science, and also that illustrations from the physical and biological sciences would often have conveyed with greater clarity the methodological principles involved. However, in a text for sociology students, the details of philosophy of science are out of place, and many of the points made in works on the logic and philosophy of science have little or no relevance or consequence for sociology as it is currently practiced. And it is an essential pedagogical requirement that our examples and illustrations should be taken from sociology. Actually, the time has passed when sociology students learn scientific method by examples from physics and other so-called established sciences. By now, sociology itself is established, and it has become varied and sophisticated enough to provide the illustrations we need for the study of principles of theory construction and theory verification.

Gothenburg in April 1963.

HANS L. ZETTERBERG
*Columbia University*

# Chapter I

# On Theoretical Sociology

In our childhood many of us enjoyed reading some popular book in physics containing chapters called, "Automobiles", "Aeroplanes", "Radios", Guns", etc. In high school, however, our physics tests did not have these titles. Now the chapter headings were, "Mechanics", "Optics", "Thermo-dynamics", etc., and the cars, planes, radios, and guns occurred only as illustrations of the principles valid in these various branches of physics. The remarkable accomplishments of physical scientists made it possible to describe all the phenomena of the physical world in terms of a limited number of laws, which we call the theories of physics. We learned these theories, and had compact descriptions of the operations of planes, radios, guns, and many other things.

We may also say that these theories became the explanation of our childhood wonders. As is well known, we explain something by demonstrating that it follows the laws of other phenomena. To ask for an explanation in science is to ask for a theory. A theory, thus, is a sword that cuts two ways. On the one hand, it is a system of information-packed descriptions of what we know; on the other hand, it is a system of general explanations. No further justification has to be given for interest in theories: the quest for informative description is the quest for theory, and the quest for explanation is a quest for theory.

Of course, we may also ask for the explanation of a theory. This desire can be answered only to the extent that we know of a more inclusive theory—sometimes called "grand theory"—of which the former is a special case. In physics, the theory of relativity and the quantum theory are inclusive theories in terms of which most laws of physics can be explained. Since they explain most laws they can also explain most phenomena. The final goal of the scientific enterprise is to know such a theory. This grand theory, however, cannot be explained. In the face of such a theory our curiosity rests.

In sociology there have been several efforts to write grand theory, but they have been judged premature by the profession. The typical strategy among contemporary sociologists was formulated by Robert K. Merton in a plea for "theories of the middle-range".[1] These are miniature theories, not grand theories; or, better expressed, partial theories rather than inclusive theories. When we call a theory partial (or middle-range, or miniature) we admit that there are other accepted theories which are not contradicted by, or synonomous with, the one we call partial. Optics and thermodynamics are examples of partial theories in physics. In social psychology, anthropology, and sociology we also have a few such theories: *e.g.*, Festinger's theory of cognitive dissonance, Homans' theory of elementary social behavior, Murdock's theory of kinship structures, Pareto's theory of elites. Sociology is believed to advance most rapidly by developing a large array of such partial theories.

At the horizon of sociological thought looms the challenging issue of integrating these partial theories into a more inclusive whole. The plea for theories of the middle-range would be misguided if it implied a condemnation of all efforts towards an inclusive theory. If inclusiveness is considered a matter of degree, it becomes again a manageable goal. (Inclusiveness is, indeed, a matter of degree: a theory can be more inclusive than another and yet be a partial theory in regard to a third theory). Steps toward inclusiveness comprising integration of two or more partial theories should be encouraged; herein lies one of the greatest challenges of the theoretical undertaking.

In sum, there is room for two types of specialists in theoretical

---

[1] Robert K. Merton, *Social Theory and Social Structure*, revised and enlarged edition, (Glencoe, Ill.: The Free Press, 1957), pp. 5-10.

sociology: the man who develops new partial theories out of his own or other people's research, and the man who takes a number of partial theories developed by others and integrates them into a more inclusive theory.

In spite of the fact that we have examples of partial theories and recognize that their integration into a more inclusive theory is a possibility, the dominant impression in looking at the sociology of today is one of theoretical paucity. We have read, in college or privately, some more or less popular texts of sociology. These texts contained chapter headings like "The Family," "Social Class," "Public Opinion," "Race Relations," etc. They dealt with the rather interesting, but theoretically unconnected, topics traditionally assigned to departments of sociology. They were more like our childhood popular physics books than the systematic physics texts of our later schooling. Present sociological thinking has rather little to offer the student who wants to go beyond this topical study to explain family structure, social class, public opinion, race relations, and other topics in terms of a few laws of sociology.

There is, however, an impressive amount of research done which gives knowledge about all these sociological topics. This flow of research findings, in fact, has become so great that it is now a losing game to try to keep abreast of all the findings. Monographs, journal articles, research proposals, mimeographed reports overtake man. To be a social theorist rather than a social researcher is no refuge from the flow of research. The days are gone when "theory" and "speculation" meant the same thing and the theorist did not have to know anything except the location of the space bar on his typewriter. Generally speaking, the modern theorist, as we visualize him, has to know more empirical findings than the most down-to-earth researcher, since he is concerned with the systematization of the knowledge researchers have acquired. As mentioned, the outcome of his labor is in the form of documents that summarize the past discoveries and events in law-like statements. We note with gratification that we now have obtained a few such research-grounded theories in the field of sociology. But we also note that most work in theoretical sociology remains to be done.

Of the elders in the field, hardly anyone has devoted himself wholly to the task of theoretical sociology. It is understandable that one of the first sociological theoreticians in the modern sense, Vilfredo Pareto, did not begin his work in theoretical sociology until he was over fifty years old.[2] It is a sadder commentary that, fifty years later, a representative theoretician, George C. Homans, who received his training and had his career at one of the world's best universities, confesses not only other pursuits prior to his endeavor in theoretical sociology, but also to a long process of unlearning of fettering traditional approaches to social thought.[3] Some fortunate members of the generation now being trained in sociology will be the first ever to orient themselves from the very start of their careers toward actual theory construction.

CURRENT MEANINGS OF SOCIAL THEORY

The conception of theory we have outlined has not been a widespread one among sociologists active in the first half of the twentieth century. One should, therefore, be aware of some older meanings of "social theory."

One of the odd habits of sociologists is to designate all of the better sociological writings of older vintage as "social theory." Statistical studies of suicide, historical studies of the effect of religion on the economy, informal observations on the role of secrets in social life, and anything else written at least a generation ago is likely to be called "social theory," if the work is good enough to live in the memory of contemporary sociologists and to be read and cited by them. An alternative (and better) term than "theory" for this material would be "sociological classics." Thus a well-known recent anthology entitled *Theories of Society*[4] contains mostly classical passages of sociological literature.

A second common conception of "social theory" equates it with a commentary on sociological writing, usually made from an historical perspec-

---

[2] To call Vilfredo Pareto "theoretician in the modern sense" is a little arbitrary since his multi-volume treatise on sociology is mainly classificatory and taxonomical. But an earlier work of his from 1901 contains a rather full-blown propositional theory, and my introduction to the English translation of the latter claims that it is the first propositional theory in sociology. See Vilfredo Pareto, *The Rise and Fall of Elites*, (Totowa, N. J.: The Bedminster Press, 1964).

[3] See the autobiographical introduction to his collection of essays entitled *Sentiments and Activities*, (New York: The Free Press of Glencoe, 1962), pp. 1-49.

[4] Talcott Parsons, *et al.*, *Theories of Society: Foundations of Modern Sociological Theory*, 2 volumes (New York: The Free Press of Glencoe, 1961).

4

tive. "Theorists" of this variety trace continuities in the accumulation of
sociological knowledge; they discover the occasions when old wine has
been poured into new bottles and new wine into old bottles. "Theory"
here means essentially "sociological criticism." A representative anthology
containing mostly recent sociological criticism is entitled *Modern Sociological Theory in Continuity and Change.*[5]

A third conception of "social theory" is represented by an anthology
such as *Toward a General Theory of Action.*[6] The task of the writers of
this book is to develop an orderly schema of anything to which sociologists (and other social scientists) should pay attention. Names are
assigned to these subjects, and the reader is encouraged to go out and
discover their concrete manifestations in all parts of society. A more
specific term than "theory" for this enterprise is "sociological taxonomy."
The anthology mentioned contains mostly suggestions for a general
taxonomy of the social sciences.

Concern with sociological classics, sociological criticism, and sociological taxonomy are all to the good. I, for one, enjoy pursuing these
interests in my teaching and writing. However, in this book, I want to
pursue sociological theory in the sense of systematically organized, law-
like propositions about society and social life. As a reminder that this is
a different breed of animal I shall speak of it as "theoretical sociology"
rather than "social theory". This speech habit is meaningless in itself, but
I believe it will serve a good purpose. Let us spell out in some further
detail how this theoretical sociology differs from sociological taxonomy.

THE TAXONOMICAL AND THE THEORETICAL APPROACH

An initial difficulty for the sociological theorist is, as mentioned, the
great variety and complexity of phenomena with which his discipline
customarily deals. As we noted, the topics have a wide range: family
discord, social mobility, labor-management relations, propaganda, public

---

[5] Howard Becker and Alvin Boskoff (eds.), *Modern Sociological Theory: In Continuity and Change,* (New York: The Dryden Press, 1957).
[6] Talcott Parsons and Edward A. Shils (eds.), *Toward A General Theory of Action,*
(Cambridge: Harvard University Press, 1959).

opinion, crime, housing, rural-urban migration, race relations, and a series of technical subjects related to the organizations and institutions of government, industry, business, education, art, religion, welfare, civic affairs, mass-media, and others. It is easy to argue that no man knows enough or is wise enough to deal with all these phenomena.

There have been times when sociology was imperialistic enough to claim all aspects of all societal phenomena as its proper realm. But the expanding scientific knowledge about society can never be the monopoly of any one academic discipline. It is a joint enterprise of historians, economists, political scientists, demographers, sociologists, anthropologists, geographers, and others. The sociologists hold only a few of the pieces to the picture puzzle of society. Specialization is necessary. Sociology, too, is a specialized science.

These two statements—that sociology deals with just about every social phenomenon, and that sociology is but a specialized one of the many social sciences—do not complement each other. How can sociology deal with everything and yet be a specialized science of the social world? Or how can sociology be a specialized social science and yet deal with all societal phenomena? The diversity of subject-matter and the necessity for specialization pose a dilemma.[7]

In principle, the resolution of the dilemma does not appear difficult. No science seems to deal with *all* aspects of what common sense considers one phenomenon. In a recent text in sociology, beginning students are given a clear demonstration of this:

> Consider your instructor's chair. If a specialist in the branch of physics called mechanics were to study it, he would see it as a combination of weights and balances; a biologist specializing in anatomy would see it as a receptacle for the human form and might assess its effect on the spinal column; an economist might see it as a product of mass production, a unit of cost and price; the psychologist might see it as a part of the perceptual frame of the student; and the sociologist might see in the chair a symbol of status. Like any field of inquiry, sociology is selective in its approach.[8]

Thus the specialization of sociology lies in its concentration on certain aspects of any social problem or any social institution, not in an in-

[7] *Cf.* Robert S. Lynd, *Knowledge for What?*, (Princeton: Princeton University Press, 1939).

[8] Leonard Broom and Philip Selznick, *Sociology*, second ed., (Evanston: Row, Peterson and Company, 1958), p. 3.

clusive study of one or two institutions or social problems.

A *first* resolution of our dilemma is to specify a small number of definitions which delineate the few aspects of reality with which sociology deals. These definitions, broadly speaking, tell the sociologist what is important for him to pay attention to when he views a human relationship, a group, or a society. The geographer, armed with definitions such as "latitude" and "longitude," looks upon a given area of the earth in these terms, but can leave such problems as the age of the crust of the earth in a given area to a geologist. Likewise, a sociologist looking at a group in terms such as "rank" and "norms", which are among his key definitions, can leave problems of the members' "personality traits" to the psychologist, who has a series of definitions to delineate them. Most work in sociology has concentrated on the development of definitions of the descriptive categories that a sociologist is to use.

This is what we call *taxonomy*. The goal is an orderly schema for the classification and description of anything social. Thus, when faced with any subject of research, the sociologist can immediately identify its crucial aspects or variables by using his taxonomy as a kind of "shopping list." To "test" his taxonomy, he takes a fresh look at subject X and shows that the general terms defining his dimensions have identifiable counterparts in X. For example, Parsons assigns certain abstract attributes to a social system, and then turns to economy, for instance, and finds that economic thinking takes these dimensions into account. He concludes that the economy is a social system. This is occasionally called to "derive" X, or "explain" X—speech habits which are rather misleading; a better term is to "diagnose" X. To make a sociological *diagnosis* of the subject-matter or problem X is to describe X in terms of a sociological taxonomy. For example, when Parsons and Smelser suggest that the distinction between short-term supply and demand in the economy is a special case of the distinction between performance and sanction in a social system[9] this is not a sociological derivation or explanation of supply and demand; it is a sociological diagnosis.

Taxonomies summarize and inspire *descriptive studies*. Thus Parsons' taxonomy guided Stouffer and Toby to a descriptive study which presented the distribution of some college students on the variable "particularism-universalism" defined by Parsons. This variable is one among

---

[9] Talcott Parsons and Neil J. Smelser, *Economy and Society*, (Glencoe, Ill.: The Free Press, 1956), p. 9.

7

others in a set called "the pattern-variable schema" which has proven useful in characterizing any social relation.[10] There are other general taxonomies for use in description of any group[11] and any society. Since sociology, like geology, botany, and geography, is largely a descriptive science, the importance of sociological taxonomy must be taken for granted. However, it should be emphasized again that a concern with taxonomy and descriptive studies does not furnish any explanations.

To know the labels of phenomena and to know their distribution is not to explain them. In the best case, these sets of definitions and maps of distributions leave you where Linnaeus left biology in the eighteenth century—that is, with denotations of species and studies of their distribution. When Darwin formulated the principles of the origin of any one species from others, he pushed biological thinking toward something more worthy of being called a theory. He not only formulated definitions of categories to investigate what cases fall into these categories; he formulated propositions and started to verify them. Sociological thinking, if it is to progress scientifically, is also bound to add some propositions to the already long array of definitions, and to let some of the effort now going into the making of descriptive studies be allocated to the verification of these propositions. In so doing, we should, of course, use as many of the previously formulated definitions as we can. Darwin was greatly aided by Linnaeus' definitions, and some —but not all—of Linnaeus' definitions became definitions in Darwin's theory.

A *second* and related resolution to the dilemma between diversity of subject-matter and the need for specialization enters here. It is represented by the program for sociology set forth by Georg Simmel over half a century ago:

> . . . we shall discover the laws of social forms only by collecting such societary phenomena of the most diverse contents, and by ascertaining what is common to them in spite of their diversity.[12]

The assumption here is that sociology will eventually discover a small

[10] Talcott Parsons, et al., "Values, Motives, and Systems of Action", in Parsons and Shils, *op. cit.*, pp. 76 ff and Samuel A. Stouffer and Jackson Toby, "Role Conflict and Personality", *ibid., pp.* 481-496.

[11] See, for example, Merton, *op. cit.*, pp. 308-326.

[12] Georg Simmel, "The Persistence of Social Groups," *American Journal of Sociology,* vol. 3 (1898), pp. 829-836.

number of propositions that are valid in several diverse contexts. This idea, that there are sociological propositions that hold in diverse contexts, is gradually becoming more of an established fact and less of a wishful hope. In George Homans' *The Human Group*[13] we find a few hypotheses confirmed by such diverse subject-matter as an industrial work-group, a Polynesian kinship structure, a city street gang, and a small New England community. This approach represents what we see as the main task of the sociological theorist—that is, the discovery of general propositions.

The systematically interrelated propositions that result from this effort are *theories*. Only at this stage does it make sense to speak of "testing a theory", "derivation", and—most important of all—"explanation". To "test" a theory, we check how well each of its propositions conforms to data and how well several propositions in conjunction with each other account for the outcome of a given situation. If such a "derivation" (or prediction) is successful, we call the outcome "explained"; that is, we claim that observed events conform to known propositions. Thus, Homans is able to explain the friendly feelings between brothers on the island of Tikopia by a reference to his already established proposition that a higher frequency of interaction results in a greater mutual liking.[14]

Theories summarize and inspire, not descriptive studies, but *verificational studies*—studies construed to test specific hypotheses. The number of such studies has grown to a gratifying extent in recent years, and every volume of the sociological journals seems to have at least a few articles in which the author formulates specific hypotheses and then reports data that bear on them. Later we will consider such studies in some detail. Here we may only express the hope that if the 1950's were particularly hospitable to taxonomies and descriptive studies, the 1960's may be hospitable to theories and verificational studies. The intellectual appeal and attractiveness of the theoretical sociology being developed by George Homans and the growing use of theory in applied sociology are two promising signs.[15]

---

[13] George C. Homans, *The Human Group*, (New York: Harcourt Brace & World, 1950).

[14] *Ibid.*, p. 242 ff.

[15] See George Homans, *Social Behavior: Its Elementary Forms*, (New York: Harcourt Brace & World, 1961) and Hans L. Zetterberg, *Social Theory and Social Practice*, (New York: The Bedminster Press, 1962).

The following listing of some key words may serve as a summary of the kinds of activities we have discussed:

|  | I | II |
|---|---|---|
| *Unit* | Definition | Proposition |
| *Interrelated units* | Taxonomy | Theory |
| *Application of unit to* | Diagnosis | Explanation |
| *new subject-matter* | | |
| *Research summarized by or* | Descriptive | Verificational |
| *inspired by unit* | study | study |

We can round out this listing by noting that some contemporary sociologists prefer the term "frame of reference" to our "taxonomy," and some, perhaps distressed at the corruption of the concept of social theory, prefer the term "model" to our "theory." The words used make little difference so long as we remember to keep separate the two enterprises depicted in our discussion. The balance of this book will deal with theories and verificational studies in sociology from a methodological point of view. The treatment of taxonomies and descriptive studies will be reserved for some other time.

CHAPTER II

# ON PROPOSITIONS IN SOCIOLOGY

Confronted with a proposition, we tend to ask, "What does it mean?" and "Is it true?". This chapter will deal with the former question, which we will subdivide into three separate questions: "What are the determinants and results entering the proposition?"; "What linkage is presumed between them?"; and "What is the informative value of the proposition?."

The propositions we will use as illustrations in this book are all phrased in ordinary language. In recent years it has been increasingly common to state propositions in some artificial language, such as mathematics or symbolic logic. The use of mathematics is not only an escape from the well-attested inability of many sociologists to write an attractive, literary prose. Mathematics adds precision to theory construction. We have much more explicit rules for manipulating mathematical expressions than we have for manipulating ordinary sentences.

The appropriate degree of precision for a theory must be chosen with an eye to the quality of the data submitted in its support and with another eye to the possible use of the theory in research and practice. Precision *per se* is a dubious and boring virtue. It will be some time before we have accumulated enough experience to assess the advantages and disadvantages of phrasing our theories in artificial languages.

*On Propositions in Sociology*

The present generation of theorists seems to be able to proceed without mathematics; the next generation will, in all likelihood, rely much more on it. The most fruitful compromise at present seems to be a very disciplined ordinary language in theoretical sociology, occasionally supported by mathematical expressions and graphs.

VARIATES: DETERMINANTS AND RESULTS

Propositions relate *variates* to each other. We say, "The more knowledege a man has, the higher his prestige," and have thus uttered a proposition that relates the two variates "knowledge" and "prestige" to each other. When we know or assume the direction in which the variates influence each other, we can designate one as a *determinant* (cause or independent variable) and the other as a *result* (effect or dependent variable). In our example, "knowledge" is the determinant and "prestige" the result; we get prestige from knowledge but no knowledge from prestige.

Note that we need, at the very minimum, two variates to have one proposition. Many propositions contain more than two; in sociology we have to consider it as normal that events have multiple determinants and/or multiple consequences. It is the predominance of such multivariate propositions that justify us in saying that ours is a complex field. Given this complexity, one gets understandably impatient with the number of statements in sociology including only one variate—*e.g.*, "*x* varies"—and also slightly suspicious of the unqualified propositions with two variates—*e.g.*, "if *x* varies, then *y* varies." I will not dignify one-variate statements by calling them propositions. We will not deal with them here; they belong to descriptive sociology (If the editors of the sociology journals made it a rule of thumb never to print any article presuming to give a theoretical discussion in which the conclusion is a one-variate statement, they would add scientific maturity to their product.)

Propositions with two variates are acceptable as intermediary steps in theory construction even if they do not tell the whole story. Once formulated they lend themselves to amendments. For example, Homans' two-variate proposition, "if the frequency of interaction between two or more persons increases, the degree of their liking of one another will increase and vice versa"[1] was a good start, even though later theorizing makes it plain that two additional variates have to be introduced—*viz.* cost of avoiding interaction, and availability of alternative rewards. A woman suffering punishment in her interaction with her husband may not break off the relation because of the high cost of divorce; but her liking for her husband does not increase as their interaction goes on. And if she finds her husband's behavior at least in part punishing but does not have an alternative man around the corner who would be more rewarding, she may continue to interact with her husband without liking him more.

Malewski adds these factors into a new formulation of the proposition: "If the costs of avoiding interaction are low, and if there are available alternative sources of reward, the more frequent the interaction, the greater the mutual liking."[2] This is a multivariate proposition, and more adequate than the original one with only two variates. However, it is not likely that one would have arrived at the multivariate one without having the two-variate one as a convenient intermediary step. Two-variate propositions can thus be justified on tactical grounds. From a pedagogical point of view, two-variate propositions are also useful, since they are so easy to grasp. Since our purpose in this book is pedagogical, it is perhaps understandable that many of our examples will contain only two variates.

The first requirement of a proposition is that the determinants and the results be precisely defined. A celebrated monograph that has been subject to much misunderstanding because it fails to state precisely its key position is Max Weber's *The Protestant Ethic and the Spirit of Capitalism*.[3] Its proposition is hinted in its very title: the Protestant ethic is the determinant and the spirit of capitalism is the result. There are, however, at least four different ways of specifying the determinant and the result in this proposition. If the terms in italics stand for the variables that may be related, we have these possibilities:

---

[1] George C. Homans, *The Human Group, op. cit.* p. 112.

[2] Andrzej Malewski, "Levels of Generality in Sociological Theory" in Hans L. Zetterberg and Gerda Lorenz (eds.), *A Symposium on Theory and Theory Construction in Sociology*, (Totowa, N. J.: The Bedminster Press, 1964).

[3] Max Weber, *Die Protestantische Ethik und der Geist des Kapitalismus* in *Gesammelte Aufsätze zur Religionssoziologie*, Vol. I (Tübingen: J. C. B. Mohr, 1922).

On Propositions in Sociology

1. The *Protestant* Ethic and the Spirit of *Capitalism*
2. The Protestant *Ethic* and the Spirit of *Capitalism*
3. The *Protestant* Ethic and the *Spirit* of Capitalism
4. The Protestant *Ethic* and the *Spirit* of Capitalism

If we emphasize the first mode, we study the frequency with which persons who are Protestants become capitalists and compare it with the frequency with which persons who are Catholics become capitalists. If the second interpretation is made, we look for ethical precepts in Protestantism which are more conducive to the emergence of capitalism than the corresponding precepts of Catholic ethics—for example, the more lenient attitude of the Protestants toward usury. If the third interpretation is made, we look for a different spirit of entrepreneurship and hard work among Protestants compared with Catholics. If the fourth interpretation is made, we presume that some ethical precepts in Protestantism, such as its invisible stratification in religion and ethics (*i.e.* the concept of predestination and the denial of good works as a measure of one's ethical worth), lead to a particular spirit which is manifested as concern with one's rank in the more visible aspects of stratification—that is, with achievements in the worlds of money, power, and science. All four ways of interpreting the thesis are in varying degrees present in Weber. Also, Weber's critics often touch upon some of these ways of interpreting the theris in a haphazard way. Thus, claims by his critics that Weber has been proven right or proven wrong are usually restricted to one or two of these possibilities. Much confusion could have been avoided if the determinant and the result of the proposition had been more clearly specified.

THE VARIETIES OF LINKAGE BETWEEN DETERMINANTS AND RESULTS

In Weber's proposition, as in most sociology, the relation between determinant and result is left vague: it is said that the Protestant ethic "leads to" or "contributed to" or was "functional" for the spirit of capitalism. In stricter theorizing we must spell out in greater detail what kind of relation is assumed in a given proposition. The topic of

14

causal linkages is complicated, and it would carry us too far from the everyday problems of the working theorist in sociology to give it a systematic presentation. Instead we will present a mere listing of varieties of causal linkage encountered in sociology and illustrate them with examples. Several of these varieties would have to be treated as being on different levels in a more systematic presentation.

A relation may be *reversible* (if X, then Y; and if Y, then X) or *irreversible* (if X, then Y; but if Y, then no conclusion about X.) Reversible propositions are not unusual in sociology. A well-known one is Homans' previously mentioned law about frequency of interaction and liking: the higher the frequency of interaction between two or more persons, the greater their liking for one another, and conversely, the greater the liking for one another among two or more persons, the higher the frequency of their interaction.[4] When we say that a proposition is reversible, we assume, in fact, that it contains two separate ideas requiring two separate tests.

Second, a relation may be *deterministic* (if X, then always Y) or *stochastic* (if X, then probably Y). Deterministic relations seem very rare in sociology. A possible example might be given by Simmel's proposition: if there is an increase in the number of members in a completely unstructured group, then there is always an increase in the anonymity of the actions of the group.[5] Stochastic relations are more common, and they range from quite strong ones to highly attenuated ones. Consider, for instance, this hypothetical statement: if a person must choose between conforming to a norm and abandoning a high rank, he is likely to keep the high rank. There are, of course, many men who would choose to obey the norm in such a dilemma, but in a large aggregate of men a majority is predicted to deviate from the norm and keep the rank.

Third, the relation may be a *sequential* one (if X, then later Y) or a *coextensive one* (if X, then also Y). An illustration of the former might be Lazarsfeld's cross-pressure proposition: if voters are subject to contradictory influences in their primary groups during an election campaign, then they are likely to delay their voting decision.[6] A coex-

---

[4] George C. Homans, *op. cit.*

[5] Georg Simmel, *Soziologie*, 3rd ed., (Berlin: Duncker & Humblot, 1923 [1958], ch. 2.

[6] Paul F. Lazarsfeld, et. al., *The People's Choice*, 2nd ed., (New York: Columbia University Press, 1948). pp. 59-61.

15

tensive relation is illustrated by the statement: The higher the rate of social mobility, the less the extent to which the lower classes accept militant class ideology.[7] No assumption is made here that mobility occurred before or after the spread of a working-class ideology. (It might be noted in passing that reversible coextensive relations are often called "functional" ones. In sociology, however, "functionalism" has so many special meanings that I will not use the word "functional" in this context.)

Fourth, a relation may be *sufficient* (if X, then Y, regardless of anything else) or *contingent* (if X, then Y, but only if Z). Sufficient propositions are rare in sociology, and contingent propositions are the rule. This is one way in which multivariate propositions dominate over two-variate propositions. For instance, all propositions about interpersonal influence assume some kind of interpersonal contact (*e.g.*, social visibility) to be valid.

Fifth, a relation may be *necessary* (if X, then, and only then, Y) or *substitutable* (if X, then Y; but if Z, then also Y). Halévy appears to assume that the presence of groupings located between the state and the family, such as non-conformist sects, was a necessary factor in the process that spared England from the bourgeois revolutions that occurred in France and other parts of Europe.[8] Propositions with substitutable determinants are otherwise very common in sociology, as seen in the wide usage of the phrase "functional equivalence." For example, in work groups paid on a piece-rate basis, we find that norms prescribing restriction of output and norms prescribing secrecy about earnings and production records may be functional equivalents in one specific sense: both are likely to reduce interpersonal tensions resulting from invidious comparisons of work achievements.

Any proposition may now be characterized according to the above check list of attributes. For example, Max Weber's thesis about a relation between the Protestant ethic and the spirit of capitalism is best interpreted as an irreversible, stochastic, sequential, contingent, and substitutable proposition.

The above five attributes of a casual relation are well known in any

---

[7] Werner Sombart, *Warum gibt es in den Vereinigten Staaten keinen Sozialismus?*, (Tübingen: J. C. B. Mohr, 1906).

[8] Eli Halévy, *Historie du peuple anglais au XIX çiècle: L'Angleterre en 1915*, 2nd ed., (Paris: Hachette, 1913).

science. Sociologists, however, might take special pains in identifying an additional type of relation. It is actually a combination of a reversible, sequential, and contingent relation, but it is so uniquely applicable to sociological subject-matter that it deserves a special name and a separate discussion. It is *interdependent* relation.

Let $\triangle x$ and $\triangle y$ be small increments in variables x and y, respectively. An interdependent relation is present when the following conditions are met:

If x changes from $x_1$ to $x_2$, and $x_2 = x_1 + \triangle x$, then and only then, y changes from $y_1$ to $y_1 + \triangle y$; further, when y changes from $y_1$ to $y_2$ and $y_2 = y_1 + \triangle y$, then and then only, x changes from $x_2$ to $x_2 + \triangle x$, etc.

Thus, in an interdependent relation, a small increment in one variable results in a small increment in a second variable; then, the increment in the second variable makes possible a further increment in the first variable which in turn affects the second one, and so this process goes on until no more increments are possible. Note, however, that an immediate large change in one variable will not bring about a large change in the other variable. The only way a large change is brought about in an interdependent relation is through a series of interacting small changes. It is as if the two variables are flirting with each other; an almost imperceptible hint, which in turn gives the first and necessary encouragement for a braver hint, and so on. A big initial hint, however, would have no effect.

The operations of an interdependent relation are found in many social processes. It is said, for example, that voluntary associations develop with the urbanization and industrialization of a society. Migration to cities creates tensions for the former rural resident which are resolved by his membership in a voluntary association, and the latter makes him a more involved urbanite and industrial employee, which in turn generates further tensions and further involvement in voluntary associations. Thus membership in voluntary associations and participation in urban and industrial life stand in a kind of piecemeal give-and-take relation that we call an interdependent relation.

The types of causal linkage should be kept in mind in all manipulations of propositions. So long as all propositions used in our theorizing are of the same type, there are few dangers involved. However, when they are of different varieties, pitfalls appear; and one must proceed with caution.

17

On Propositions in Sociology

## FUNCTIONAL PROPOSITIONS

No review of varieties of sociological propositions would be complete without a mention of the common practice of making a functional assessment of propositions. Many times sociologists use the word "function" meaning only "result" and the term "functional prerequisite" meaning only "determinant." However, in stricter thinking, "function" has a more special meaning:

> Functions are those observed consequences which make for the adaptation or adjustment of a given system; and dysfunctions, those observed consequences which lessen the adaptation of the system.[9]

In an analysis of the functionalist position, Galtung points out that the crucial words in this statement by Merton are "adaptation" and "adjustment":

> But "adaptation" and "adjustment" to what? The answer "to S [the system] as it is, to status quo" can be discarded at once—this would make all consequences implying social change dysfunctional by definition. The answer "to a social change in or of S" can likewise be discarded, as we do not believe today that consequences implying social change are necessarily beneficial for the system.[10]

Galtung proceeds to give the answer in terms of some shared value within a subsystem. By voluntarily keeping their output roughly at the same modest level, workers paid according to piece rates do not envy each other's take-home pay, and they help preserve well-paying piece-rate contracts. Expressed as a functional proposition this would read: The functions of informal norms prescribing restriction of output are to reduce invidious comparisons of wages, and to keep stable, high wages. Both these functions can be justified by values held by the majority of the workers, but not by the values held by the majority of employers; the latter want maximum output for the lowest possible

[9] Robert K. Merton, *Social Theory and Social Structure*, revised and enlarged edition (Glencoe, Ill.: The Free Press, 1957), p. 51.

[10] Johan Galtung, "An Outline of Structural-Functional Theory Applied to Social Change", unpublished manuscript, Ch. I, p. 6.

18

wage costs. What is functional and dysfunctional thus depends on the values in the social system or subsystem taken as a point of departure.

Before accepting this radical solution, it may be appropriate to consider the use of functionalism in other fields. Professor Nagel sums up a review of functionalist formulations in various sciences in the following way:

> Accordingly, functional statements are regarded as appropriate in connection with systems possessing self-maintaining mechanisms for certain of their traits, but seem pointless and even misleading when used with reference to systems lacking such self-regulatory devices.[11]

This makes sociological functionalism dependent on the discovery of self-regulatory mechanisms that keep a given variable at a certain level or "goal state," in Nagel's terminology. Those factors are "functional" which keep a variable at the goal state, while those factors that tend to move it from the goal are "dysfunctional." Biology can demonstrate many such goal states, which are maintained within very narrow limits, for example, the sugar level in the blood. Whether sociology will discover some is an open question.

Two less rigid aspects of functionalism are illustrated in the works of Talcott Parsons. He hypothesizes that all social systems (and all subsystems, etc.) have to solve four problems: (1) "adaptation," (2) "goal-attainment," (3) "integration," and (4) "latent-pattern maintenance and tension management." These are the "functional imperatives" of any system of action.[12] Imagine that we can measure how well each is resolved in a social system by reading four master gauges, and that all subsystems have similar gauges; and that we also can rate the subsystems according to the input and output they make of these four quantities in the larger system. Each gauge will now have at its lower end a red danger zone; if the dial on any one of the four master gauges falls in this danger zone, Parsons would predict that the whole system would perish. The same would be the case with a subsystem if any of its four gauges fell below their critical points; the larger system would still remain, but only if the disappearance of the input contributed by the subsystem does not reduce the quantities necessary to maintaining

11 Ernest Nagel, *Logic Without Metaphysics*, (Glencoe, Ill.: The Free Press, 1961), pp. 251-252.
12 Talcott Parsons, "An Outline of the Social System", Talcott Parsons, et al., (eds.) in *Theories of Society*, Vol. I, (Glencoe, Ill.: The Free Press, 1961), pp. 38-41.

the larger system beyond the critical point. Thus we see that the functional formulation here is applied, not as in Nagel's case involving the maintenance of a narrow range or goal state of a variable, but only in the maintenance of minimum values on variables.

The second, and more important, use of functional formulations by Parsons concerns the operation and change of on-going systems. He assumes that the reading of the dials above the danger zone would show certain interdependencies. For example, if an advance is made in adaptation—caused by added resources channeled to this area by internal or external events modifications would have to be made also in the other problem areas. Parsons has not yet written a set of specific propositions about these interdependencies, but it is clear that he .expects the quantities represented by the dials to form a moving equilibrium. Thus propositions in functional language are used here in a way that has long standing in the social sciences: that is, to specify an equilibrium theory. Whether they have an advantage over conventional propositions or equations about determinants and results, which normally are used to write equilibrium theories, remains to be seen. It should also be noted that Parsons' type of functionalism, while clearly aimed at inclusive theory, uses an approach that at best will produce a partial theory. Assuming that sociologists would agree on what are the imperative problems of any social system—itself a rather remote possibility—no assurance can be given that *all* sociological propositions are relevant to these problems. Thus there would be some sociological knowledge that is not included in the functionalist formulations.

At present, functionalist formulations enjoy wide currency in sociology. I have some misgivings as to their usefulness to the sociological *theorist,* since they assume either self-maintaining "goal states" that have not yet been discovered, or universal "imperatives" that are subject to disagreement and probably are unrelated to at least some sociological knowledge. Less doubt can exist, however, of the usefulness of functionalist formulations to the social *practitioner.* The logic of functionalism—to judge consequences in terms of "adjustment" and "adaptation," or·"goal states," or "imperative" problems specified in advance of analysis—is the typical logic of applied theory.

ORDINARY AND THEORETICAL PROPOSITIONS

To present precisely defined determinants and results and specified relations between them are two ways of answering the question: What does this proposition mean? A third way of answering the same query phrases the answer in terms of the *informative value* of the proposition.

In general, the larger the number of different ways in which a proposition can conceivably be proven incorrect, the higher its informative value. Put differently, the higher the informative value of a proposition, the greater is the variety of events for which it can account. A critical task for the theorist in any science is to subsume a large number of propositions of low informative value under a few propositions of higher informative value. When the theorist asks about a proposition, "What does it mean?", he wants to know also (1) what are the less informative propositions that are implied in the one under consideration, and (2) what are the more imformative propositions that imply the one under consideration.

Propositions of low informative value are legion, and I shall simply call them *ordinary* propositions. Propositions of high informative value deserve to be called *theoretical* propositions.

Since theoretical sociology is already very abstract, it is essential for both researchers and practitioners to learn to extract the ordinary propositions from theoretical ones. Researchers need them for their research designs, and practitioners need them as bases for concrete advice to clients.

Suppose we ask for the ordinary propositions implied in this theoretical one:

> Persons tend to engage in actions that maintain the evaluations they
> receive from their associates.

A key term here is 'evaluations.' Like so many other terms in sociology, it is a broad tent covering a multitude of phenomena that look different to common sense. We find the special cases of this proposition by searching in our taxonomy for all terms that have 'evaluations' as a component. We find, among many others, that 'approval' is defined as an evaluation of an action; 'esteem' is defined as an evaluation of a person; and 'rank' is defined as an evaluation of a position in a social structure. We can now specify our proposition so that it deals separately with these three instances. For example, the last of the three propositions so obtained would read:

> Persons tend to engage in actions that maintain the rank they enjoy in their social structure.

This is the well-known story that men tend to do everything to avoid demotion.

We may proceed further by decomposing terms other than evaluation in our original proposition. Suppose we take the term 'action.' One taxonomy divides it into 'physical actions' and 'communicative actions,' and the latter in turn into 'descriptions' ("Mr. X is a Senator") 'evaluations' ("Mr. X is a great man") and 'prescriptions' ("Re-elect Senator X!"). This sensitizes us to the variety of actions that may be involved in maintaining approval, esteem, and rank. To single out just one of the many propositions specifying each variety of evaluation, we take the category of evaluation we last discussed and the last category of action, and obtain the following:

> Persons tend to issue prescriptions that maintain the rank they enjoy in their social structure.

In other words, a person would try to issue rules that help him retain tenure in his rank.

We may further decompose the term 'social structure,' for example, into 'organization,' structures with common leadership, and 'markets,' structures without common leadership. The latter could be further broken down into markets in various institutional reals, *e.g.* economic markets such as commodity exchanges, scientific markets such as fields of social science, political markets such as electorates, *et cetera*. Taking only the last-mentioned as an illustration, we have:

> Persons tend to issue prescriptions that maintain the rank they enjoy in their electorate.

Thus, if a person has any elected rank at all, he will work for those rules, suggestions, and laws that maintain him in office. This proposition of political sociology is thus a special case of our original theoretical one.

We may proceed to apply it to a specific electorate, *e.g.* the American, to specific persons, *e.g.* the House of Representatives, at a specific time, *e.g.* 1963. This gives us one of the necessary propositions for relating the work of the 88th Congress to the sentiments of the American people. We have gone from the theoretical to the ordinary.

The type of causal linkage in the special case is the same as in the original proposition. If we assumed that the original proposition was an irreversible, stochastic, coextensive, sufficient one, then its ordinary implications would have the same causal linkage.

If we want to investigate whether two or more ordinary propositions can be assumed under the same theoretical proposition, we first must establish whether they have the same type of causal linkage. If such a similarity in type can reasonably be assumed, we may proceed by analyzing the *terms* in the ordinary propositions which indicate their determinants and results. If these terms have common elements, we can then formulate a theoretical proposition by using these common elements. An illustration may clarify this procedure.

Suppose we have the following findings:

> Students at Bennington College in the middle 1930's who were elected worthy by popular vote of representing the school in a meeting with other colleges were more affected by the liberal values predominant among their teachers and fellow students than were others.[13]

> Subjects in a social psychological experiment in Ann Arbor in the late 1940's who were told that their instructor-experimenter selected them as a model group agreed with each other in the writing of a story connecting three pictures more than did others who were not told that they were a model group.[14]

From reading the studies by Newcomb and by Back which report these findings, it seems reasonable to assume that we have in both instances a stochastic substitutable proposition, contingent on social visibility of attitudes and cognitions. It is less easy to say from the studies whether the findings are sequential or coextensive, reversible or irreversible. My

---

[13] Theodore M. Newcomb, *Personality and Social Change*, (New York: Dryden Press, 1943).
[14] Kurt Back, "Influence through Social Communication", *Journal of Abnormal and Social Psychology*, Vol. 46 (1951), pp. 9-23.

On Propositions in Sociology

guess would be that they are reversible and coextensive. I shall, however, assume that whatever one is, the other is the same.

The findings state that whatever happened took place in "a college" and in a "social psychological experiment," among "students" and "teachers" in one instance and "subjects" and "instructor-experimenter" in the other instance. We subsume college and social psychological experiment under the term "group" and all the persons involved under the term "group member." If a single theoretical proposition can be found that implies the two findings, it will be one that deals with groups and group members. However, all measures were taken among the rank-and-file members of the groups (the students), so the effects should be stated as valid only for the rank-and-file.

We now analyze the determinants in the findings. They are:

"elected worthy by popular vote of representing the school in a meeting with other colleges"

"told that their instructor-experimenter had selected them as a model group . . ."

Both of these may be subsumed under:

"received more favorable evaluations."

Proceeding to the results we have in the findings:

"more affected by the liberal values predominant"

"agreed with each other more in writing a story"

Both of these may be assumed under:

"their ideas converged more with those of other group members."

We can now formulate a theoretical proposition which contains our two findings:

The more favorable evaluations rank-and-file members receive in a group, the more their ideas converge with those of other group members.

We have gone from the ordinary to the theoretical. The resulting proposition, like its component findings, is assumed to be a stochastic, contingent one with a substitutable determinant.

Note that in the process of formulating the theoretical proposition we dropped references to Bennington and Ann Arbor and to the fact that the studies were made in the 1930's and 40's. In highly theoretical propositions we do not make references to time and space; these propositions are presumed valid in all places at all times. Nor do they contain proper names (*e.g.* of specific individuals); they are presumed valid for all.

In reviewing our illustration, it is clear that we arrived at our theoretical proposition by a process of analyzing terms used in the findings. If we had had no terminological schema into which the words of our findings could have been fitted, it would have been difficult to arrive at the theoretical proposition. Here, then, is a type of problem whose solution requires a good taxonomy.

# Chapter III

# The Ordering Of Sociological Propositions

Any sociological topic is likely to bring to mind many propositions. These propositions are identified and presented in a variety of ways in theoretical publications. Some writers present them in the normal course of a paragraph, and the reader is warned merely by the surrounding text that a proposition has been advanced. Some authors help their readers by presenting their propositions in italics. Still others set them apart by indentations or other typographical devices. Some present them as listings under special subheadings such as "Hypotheses." Many give them numbers or proper names to facilitate their identification. No uniform rules prevail here, nor are they needed so long as the reader is made aware that certain sentences are propositions.

Regardless of how propositions are identified, the problem of ordering them becomes important as soon as they reach a number beyond two or three. While it is possible to simply list the propositions—as do the authors of *Voting* in a useful appendix—more efficient modes of ordering propositions are often possible. Let us illustrate some currently used formats.

26

INVENTORY OF DETERMINANTS

All factors that affect a certain phenomenon are systematically listed in an inventory of determinants. A good issustration is provided in a paper by Kingsley Davis and Judith Blake containing propositions of factors determining a society's fertility rate.[1] The factors are sorted into three main categories: (1) those affecting the likelihood of sexual intercourse, (2) those affecting the likelihood of conception, and (3) those affecting the likelihood of fetus survival. Each one is subdivided to allow formulation of specific propositions. The first category contains a variety of propositions:

1.  The higher the customary age for entry into marriage (or other sexual union), the lower the fertility rate.

    For example, property rules in Ireland, where a father relinquishes control over farm property at his son's marriage, is conducive to a high age at marriage (29 years for women) and this factor depresses the fertility rate.

2.  The greater proportion of women in permanent celibacy, the lower the fertility rate.

    For example, the low proportion of never-married women in Ceylon (.8%) and India (3.4%) make for high fertility, while the high proportion in Ireland (26.3%) or Sweden (20.9%) leads to a low fertility rate.

3.  The longer the time of celibacy, after or between unions, the lower the fertility rate.

    For example, prohibition of remarriage of widows and divorcées in some societies or religions depresses the fertility rate. The time-lapses between common-law marriages for women in Jamaica reduces the fertility rate by 37%.

And so the authors continue to develop over a dozen propositions in which the the determinants (independent variables) vary but the result (dependent variable) is always fertility.

---

[1] Kingsley Davis and Judith Blake, "Social Structure and Fertility: An Analytic Framework", *Economic Development and Cultural Change*, Vol. 5 (1956), pp. 211-235.

*The Ordering of Sociological Propositions*

## INVENTORY OF RESULTS

A list of propositions in which the determinant is one and the same but the dependent variables are different is an inventory of results. An illustration is furnished by Janowitz in a paper on the consequences of mobility.[2] The author organizes his propositions into two categories: (1) those dealing with consequences for primary groups, and (2) those dealing with consequences for secondary groups. To sample:

> The greater the social mobility of a family, the greater the instability of a family.
>
> The greater the social mobility of a person, the stronger his ethnic and racial prejudices.
>
> Upward mobility produces the political behavior typical of the new (higher) stratum.
>
> Downward mobility produces the political behavior typical of the old (higher) stratum.

Janowitz is able to show that all propositions about mobility and primary groups can be subsumed under one more informative proposition first suggested by Durkheim: "Increased social mobility leads to increased disruption of primary relations." No such theoretical proposition can subsume his statements about the consequences of mobility on secondary groups.

## CHAIN PATTERNS OF PROPOSITIONS

When we deal with two or more sequential propositions in which a result in one reappears as a determinant in another, we can order them as a chain. An illustration is furnished by Terence Hopkins,[3] who has

---

[2] Morris Janowitz, "Some Consequences of Social Mobility in the United States", *Transactions of the Third World Congress of Sociology*, Vol. 3 (1956), pp. 191-201.

[3] Terence K. Hopkins, *The Exercise of Influence*, (Totowa, N. J.: The Bedminster Press, 1964).

reviewed studies of small groups, focusing, among other things, on four aspects:

a. The *knowledge* possessed by a person of the needs and attitudes of other group members;
b. The *prestige* of a person, that is, the extent to which others give him a favorable evaluation;
c. The *authority* of a person, that is, the extent to which he issues directions to the group acceptable to the group members;
d. The *centrality* of a person in the group, that is, the extent to which he maintains interaction with many other group members.

Studies can be cited showing that all these variables are positively correlated. If a person possesses one of these attributes he is likely to possess the others as well. Twelve separate propositions—or, better, six reversible propositions—can be written to show these relations.

However, the studies make it reasonable to assume that we deal here with sequential propositions. One possible flow of determinants and result is the following:

1. Persons who occupy *central* positions, that is, interact with many other group members, tend to obtain a better *knowledge* of their needs and attitudes;
2. Persons who have better *knowledge* of the needs and attitudes of others can more easily issue directives acceptable to others and thus tend to obtain higher *authority;*
3. Persons of higher *authority* tend to receive more *prestige;*
4. Persons with *prestige* become sought-after interaction partners, and thus tend to obtain *central* positions in the group.

Chains like these can be illustrated by a schema of arrows:

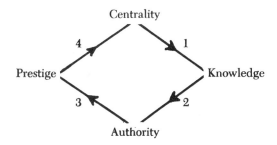

One should not expect that every chain in this way becomes a circle; all kinds of geometric patterns are possible. Even for the problem at hand Hopkins has suggested several alternatives.

Chain patterns of great complevity can be simulated by electronic calculators. I will not discuss this here, except by noting that electronic simulations are most useful when we deal with complex patterns of causal linkages of the sequential type. Their usefulness when the causal linkages are of other types is less certain.

MATRIXES OF PROPOSITIONS

Another form of presenting propositions is the matrix. Here a certain number of factors are given and all their interrelations are specified. An example is furnished by the early part of Homans' book, *The Human Group*. Three variables are given: "activity," "interaction," and "sentiment." They are all considered both as determinants and results. Thus we get the matrix:

|  |  | Results | | |
|---|---|---|---|---|
|  |  | Activity | Interaction | Sentiment |
|  | Activity | --- | $H_{ai}$ | $H_{as}$ |
| Determinants | Interaction | $H_{ia}$ | --- | $H_{is}$ |
|  | Sentiment | $H_{sa}$ | $H_{si}$ | --- |

In various parts of his text Homans can then spell out the six possible interrelations between these variables. They happen to be three reversible propositions, presumably of a coextensive type:

$H_{is}$ and $H_{si}$:  "If the frequency of interaction between two or more persons increases, the degree of their liking [sentiment] for one another will increase, and vice versa"[4]

$H_{ai}$ and $H_{ia}$:  "If the scheme of activities is changed, the scheme of interaction will, in general, also change, and vice versa"[5]

---

[4] George C. Homans, *The Human Group*, (New York: Harcourt Brace & World, 1950), p. 112.

[5] *Ibid.* p. 102

H$_{as}$ and H$_{sa}$ :  "A motive sentiment gives rise to an activity . . . but if either side of the relationship is changed, the other will be affected"[6]

It is plain that if we read across the rows of the matrix of propositions we obtain inventories of results, for example, "if high interaction, then much activity"; "if high interaction, then much sentiment." If we read down a column we have an inventory of determinants, for example, "if much activity, then high interaction"; "if much sentiment, then high interaction." Unlike an arrow schema of a chain pattern, a matrix like this one is not restricted in its usefulness to sequential propositions.

AXIOMATIC FORMAT WITH DEFINITIONAL REDUCTION

Inventories and matrixes list every relevant proposition. A sophisticated theorist, however, might want to reduce the size of the matrix. This leads to an axiomatic theory. Axiomatic theories can have many different patterns. We shall illustrate only two possibilities, one obtained by a reduction of a matrix through the manipulation of the definitions, and one obtained through the manipulation of the propositions. Normally, both manipulations are done at the same time; however, it may be more instructive for us to discuss each separately.

A brief example of a definitional reduction in a list of propositions can be constructed on the basis of a discussion of social aggregates by Arnold Rose.[7] Let us assume as given this inventory of propositions about the emotional excitement and membership turnover in social aggregates.

1.  Groups have less turnover than publics
2.  Publics show less emotion than crowds
3.  Groups show less emotion than masses

We begin the reduction of these propositions by an analysis of the key terms:

---

[6] *Ibid.* p. 99
[7] Arnold M. Rose, *Sociology,* (New York: Alfred A. Knopf, 1954), Ch. 9.

    a. Groups are social aggregates interacting in terms of specified roles and with a common leader (e.g., a voluntary association).

    b. Masses are social aggregates interacting (if at all) in terms of unspecified roles but with a common leader (e.g., a radio audience).

    c. Publics are social aggregates interacting in terms of specified roles but without a common leader (e.g., a market).

    d. Crowds are social aggregates interacting in terms of unspecified roles and without a common leader (e.g., milling in Times Square).

Comparing these with our original propositions, we find that the aggregate with common leader is assumed to have less turnover, and the aggregates with interaction in terms of specified roles show less emotion. Thus our original propositions are reduced to two theoretical propositions:

    I. If a social aggregate has a common leader, then its turnover is low.

    II. If a social aggregate interacts in terms of specified roles, then its level of emotion is low.

The most interesting part of this procedure is that these two propositions do not merely imply the three that we had as our starting point but also a fourth. Proposition (I) and Definition (b) imply that "masses have less turnover than crowds." This is a novel hypothesis which, to the best of my knowledge, is presented here for the first time. Thus we see how an axiomatic format not merely organizes existing propositions but generates new ones implicit in the existing ones.

AXIOMATIC FORMATS WITH PROPOSITIONAL REDUCTION

In the previous example we obtained a reduction in a list of propositions by combining propositions with definitions. It is also possible to obtain a reduction by combining propositions with other propositions. From the list of original propositions (inventories or matrices) a certain number are selected as *postulates*. The postulates are chosen so that all other propositions, the *theorems*, are capable of derivation from the postulates and no postulate is capable of derivation from other postulates. One generally strives to use as few postulates a possible. Assume, for example, that the following propositions are given:

1. If national prosperity increases, then the middle classes expand.
   Economists are fairly well in agreement that the ranks of service occupations, dealers and brokers, expand during periods of prosperity and in countries with a growing GNP.

2. If the middle classes expand, the consensus of values in the society increases.
   While disproportionate expansion of lower or upper classes leads to a polarization of values (as Marx argued), a similar expansion of the middle classes promotes the convergence of values in the society.

3. If the middle classes expand, the social mobility increases.
   The expanding ranks of the middle classes must be filled by persons from other classes, thus promoting mobility.

4. If social mobility increases, the consensus of values in the society increases and *vice versa*.
   Social mobility creates families in which fathers, sons and brothers belong to different classes and family loyalties modify class ideologies. This is a reversible proposition: if there is much consensus of values between social strata, then social mobility between them becomes easier.

From this list we may select propositions (1), (2), and (4) as postulates. Let us restate them with roman numbers:

I. If national prosperity increases, the middle classes expand.

II. If the middle classes expand, the consensus on values increases.

III. If social mobility increases, the consensus on values increases, and vice versa.

The implications of these propositions can now be spelled out in the form of theorems. Postulates II and III combine into the familiar:

3. If the middle classes expand, the social mobility increases thus completing the set of propositions we had at the beginning.

in addition, Postulates I and II render this theorem:

5. If national prosperity increases, the consensus on values increases.

Furthermore, if Theorem 3 is combined with Postulate I, we obtain:

6. If national prosperity increases, the social mobility increases.

33

The last two theorems are novel in the sense that they were not included in our original set. Theorem 5 is not trivial; it suggests, for example, that if we want to promote social stability in the form of less political and ideological cleavages in a society, we should maximize its national income. (This is one way in which foreign aid to less prosperous societies may be argued.) Theorem 6 has been mentioned—in fact, among others by Lipset and myself—in the literature;[8] I was just not aware of its logical ties with our original propositions.

Our experience in axiomatizing sociological propositions is limited. However, I believe the above instances are fairly typical: attempts toward axiomatization often generate some propositions that were not explicitly mentioned in the original set. Some of these added propositions may be novel; others may be well-known by themselves but not in their connections with other propositions. An axiomatic schema renders this service because it makes visible *all* ideas implicit in *some* given ideas.

I do not hesitate, therefore, to recommend to a theorist to arrange his propositions in the axiomatic way: it forces him to spell out his assumptions, to make explicit his deductions; and it will remind him of any bypassed implications. This does not necessarily mean that his final publication should have an axiomatic organization. The way propositions are presented to the public is an editorial question. There may be instances in which axiomatic thinking is most efficient but an axiomatic editorial format becomes so cumbersome that it gets in the way of efficient communication. Theoretical sociology can never surrender logic to taste or style; however, as soon as we know from an axiomatic exposition that our logic is good, there is every reason to proceed in the best of taste and style.

---

[8] Seymour Martin Lipset and Hans L. Zetterberg, "Social Mobility in Industrial Societies" in Seymour Martin Lipset and Reinhard Bendix, *Social Mobility in Industrial Society*, (Berkeley and Los Angeles: University of California Press, 1959). p. 27.

CHAPTER IV

# THE CONFIRMATION OF A PROPOSITION

So far, we have dealt with the question of what propositions mean and how they may be ordered. Now let us turn to the equally crucial issue of the truth of the propositions, the evidence that support them.

Let us begin by noting that propositions supported by evidence are called *invariances*, and propositions for which more evidence is needed are called *hypotheses*. This distinction cross-cuts our previous one between ordinary and theoretical propositions, and we get this important four-fold division:

|  | *Low informative value* | *High informative value* |  |
|---|---|---|---|
| *Empirical support wanting* | Ordinary hypothesis | Theoretical hypothesis | **Hypotheses** |
| *Empirical support sufficient* | Ordinary invariance: Finding | Theoretical invariance: Law | **Invariances** |
|  | **Ordinary propositions** | **Theoretical propositions** |  |

*The Confirmation of a Proposition*

An ordinary invariance is what we know as a *finding;* a theoretical invariance is what we know as a *law.* (Our current speech habits do not give separate words for ordinary and theoretical hypotheses.)

There is an embarrassment of riches of ordinary hypotheses about social life. Most sociologists at present take this as a great challenge to test the hypotheses and turn them into findings of high probabilities. However, as Popper points out:

> Science does not aim, primarily, at high probabilities. It aims at high informative content, well backed by experience. But a hypothesis may be very probable simply because it tells us nothing, or very little.[1]

I think we should allow ourselves a little more courage in taking the abundance of available propositions about social life as a challenge to turn ordinary hypotheses into theoretical ones without first maximizing the evidence that supports them. This is one way in which sociology can avoid its current painstaking triviality. In particular, I think sociology should make a more serious effort to incorporate in its theories the best thoughts (theoretical hypotheses) of the human condition found in Homer, Dante, Shakespeare, Cervantes, Twain and other great writers, who now provide the lion's share of any educated layman's conception of the human drama.[2] In the end, however, the outcome of the theoretical enterprise should be "high informative content, well backed by experience," that is, laws. Only experience through trial and error can teach us whether we arrive from ordinary hypotheses to laws more easily via findings or via theoretical hypotheses. For the present, we shall only discuss how hypotheses are turned into invariances, and leave this question open.

In the last analysis, the verification enterprise is a comparison of two broad classes of sentences, those in a theory and those about indicators and data. They should not contradict each other, nor vary independently of each other, but be in consonance. It does not make any difference whether the theory has preceded the research or vice versa; which class of sentences was written first is irrelevant. But they must agree according to a set of rules that we shall try to make explicit in next chapter.

Our focus will be the confirmation of a *single* hypothesis. However, it

---

[1] Karl Popper, "Degree of Confirmation", *British Journal for the Philosophy of Science*, Vol. 6 (1955), p. 146.
[2] A successful illustration of this approach is found in Hugh Dalziel Duncan, *Communication and Social Order*, (New York: The Bedminster Press, 1962).

36

should be said at the very outset that it is virtually impossible to confirm a single hypothesis but quite possible to confirm a theory, a system of hypotheses. For pedagogical purposes, however, we may focus on a single hypothesis in this chapter, and postpone the discussion of systems of hypotheses to chapter 6.

It sounds so simple when we say that in order to confirm a hypothesis we check it against observations. However, the actual procedure is amazingly complicated, and errors of many different kinds can easily creep in and disqualify the results. Some major steps in verification will be set forth in this chapter, and some of them will receive special attention in the next chapter. We will, however, avoid treating the very intricate problem of the possibilities of induction in general. We will instead tie our treatment to some current practices among sociologists which appear sound and reasonable.

AN OVERVIEW OF STEPS IN CONFIRMING A PROPOSITION

As an illustration of the confirmation of a single proposition, let us discuss a test of the hypothesis: "The more a member conforms to the norms of a formal organization, the greater the likelihood that he will be promoted." This will be called the Conformity-Promotion Proposition. Relevant data for testing are available in *The American Soldier*.[3]

The indicators "conformity to Army norms" consist of six questions, for example: "In general, how serious an offense do you think it is for a soldier to go 'AWOL' (Absent without official leave)?" The conformist answer to this question is "very serious," while other answers were rated as non-conformist. The conformist answers to all six questions were fitted into a Guttman-type quasi-scale with a reproducibility coefficient of .82. In all, this index measuring conformity to Army norms appears valid and fairly reliable. It was part of a questionnaire given in November, 1953, to privates. According to their scores on the scale, they were classified as Strict Conformist (score 5-6), Medium Conformists (score 3-4), and Poor Conformists (score 0-2). To record "promotion", a search was made in the records to find out which of the same privates had

---

[3] Samuel A. Stouffer, et al., *The American Soldier: Adjustment during Army Life*, (Princeton: Princeton University Press, 1949, Vol. I), pp. 258-265.

made the rank of non-commissioned officer (mostly corporals) by March, 1944. There is no need to question the validity or reliability of this simple indicator. The sample consisted of 374 men from an Infantry division who had entered the Army during the summer of 1943.

We now proceed to check whether the data trend fits the trend predicted by the hypothesis. The following summary gives the necessary information:

| Conformity to Army Rules | Prediction from hypothesis: Likelihood of promotion | Per cent promoted |
|---|---|---|
| Strict conformists (N=68) | High | 31% |
| Medium conformists (N=138) | Medium | 28% |
| Poor conformists (N=112) | Low | 17% |

Thus, we find that the trend in data parallels the trend predicted from the theoretical proposition.

The fact that data and proposition point in the same direction is comforting. To be more certain, however, we might also want to appraise not only that this parallelism exists but also to what extent it exists. In our case the differences appear small, particularly between the strict and medium conformists. Ours is not precise enough to allow a strict test of the "goodness of fit"; sociological models rarely make detailed predictions about the behavior of the indicators, only over-all predictions. In our case, we can at best check how often differences of the magnitude we found occur as chance fluctuations in sampling. A chi-square test renders $X^2=5.916$, which corresponds to the probability $.05<p.<.06$ with a two-tail test of significance. This gives us only a modest assurance that that trend in our data would be replicated in new samples. The representativeness of the sample could not be checked for this particular instance, but information about similar samples in War Department studies allow us to assume that this one is fair. The scope of the population—the U. S. Army in World War II—is a more serious limitation; ideally we would like to see the proposition tested with data from other institutional realms, *e.g.* a religious hierarchy, a business enterprise, a civilian government bureaucracy, a university.

The most intriguing problem of appraising our test remains: to control for alternative explanations. We know from other parts of the Army study that likelihood of promotion increases with length of service, and that it increases with education. How can we make sure that seniority or educational qualifications (or any other known or unknown factor) cannot account for our finding? As for seniority, we know that it could not play any part, since all our subjects have been in the Army equally long. The part played by education was checked in this and two other samples through the technique of multivariate analysis.[4] The tables are not published, but the authors report the result in the text:

> When the data . . . are broken down into two educational classes, the same consistency appears in all three samples for high school graduates and college men and in two of the three samples for other men, in spite of the small number of cases.[5]

Thus we have some assurance that differences in educational qualifications do not account for the findings about likelihood of promotion. Whether other alternative factors, unknown at present, can account for the trend in our data remains a question. Only experimental designs can control for unknown alternative hypotheses.

Most research workers would probably stop their test at this point. However, one more appraisal ought to be done: how well integrated is the tested proposition in available social theory? We know from a large number of studies that the proposition "the more a member conforms to the norms of his group, the more favorable valuations does he receive from his group"[6] is valid. Let us call this the Sanction Proposition. There is also a well-known sociological proposition about rank equilibrium: a person with high rank in one sphere of life tends to move toward high ranks also in other spheres of life.[7] This proposition can be generalized into one which has higher informative value: "the more a person receives favored valuation on one dimension, the greater the likelihood that he receives favored valuations also on other dimensions." This we might call the Halo Proposition. However, "rank" is a social valuation of a position. Thus we can specify our derivation to read: "the more a member conforms to the norms of his group, the greater likeli-

[4] *Infra*. pp. 62-65.

[5] Samuel A. Stouffer, *op. cit.*, p. 263.

[6] Henry W. Riecken and George C. Homans, "Psychological Aspects of Social Structure" in G. Lindzey, *Handbook of Social Psychology*, (Cambridge, Mass.: Addison-Wesley, 1954), pp. 786-832.

[7] Emile Benoit-Smullyan, "Status, Status Types, and Status Interrelations", *American Sociological Review*, Vol. 9 (1944), pp. 151-61.

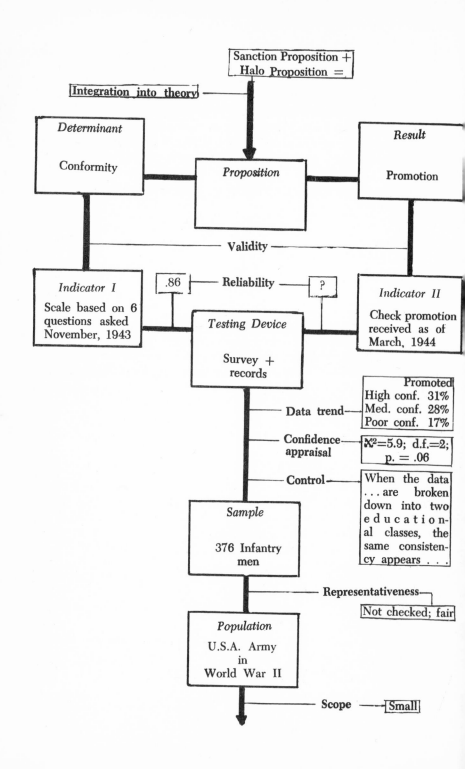

hood that he is given higher rank." Now we have only to note that a "formal organization" is a kind of group and that to be "given higher rank" is to be "promoted" and we have the proposition of our test: "the more a member conforms to the norms of a formal organization, the greater the likelihood that he will be promoted." Thus we see that the hypothesis we test is consistent with other confirmed propositions. This greatly adds to our confidence in accepting it as plausible.

The steps in our appraisal of this study are illustrated in the adjoining flow chart.

In summary, we base our decision to call the Conformity-Promotion Proposition confirmed on the following criteria:

(1) the validity of the indicators;
(2) the reliability of the indicators;
(3) the fit between the data trend from the indicators and the trend predicted by the tested proposition:
    (a) the extent the direction of the trends coincide;
    (b) the likelihood that the data trend is a chance fluctuation;
(4) the control of alternative propositions;
(5) the representativeness of the sample and the scope of the population;
(6) the extent to which the tested proposition is an integral part of established theory.

All these criteria have to be weighted into a composite judgment of acceptance or rejection. The fact that we can get quantitative estimates of criteria (2) and (3b) should not tempt us to give undue emphasis to them. The beginner would probably reject the tested hypothesis because the reproducibility .83 it not quite the desired .90, or the significance level .06 is not the customary .05 used in his textbook. In our opinion, a rejection would be a mistake. The validity seems good, the fit (3a) is fair, one important alternative hypothesis is ruled out, and the proposition is integrated in established theory. The reliability and statistical significance are not so far off that they subtract much from the good impression the test gives on these more important criteria. Thus we accept for the time being the Conformity-Promotion Proposition as tentatively confirmed.

At this point a lingering doubt might occur: should we not, after all, play it safe and reject the proposition? Even if we are 85 per cent sure, is it not correct, in the name of science, to reject it? The answer is no. Sci-

entific advance is as much hampered by the error of rejecting something true as by accepting something false.


## THE SEPARATION OF DEFINITIONS AND INDICATORS

To some writers, the confirmation procedure concerns only the indicators. It is, therefore, tempting to dispense entirely with everything
else. Why not simply call the indicators "operational definitions" and
not use any other definitions of determinants and results? This is the position taken by orthodox operationalists. This movement has been strong
in contemporary sociology and deserves some attention. Lundberg expresses its spirit when he writes about Thurstone's operational definition of attitudes:

> Thus, Thurstone records his observation of certain behavior. This
> behavior explicitly defined operationally, he calls an attitude. Where-
> upon his critics vigorously proclaim that this is not an attitude at all.
> *Attitude* is something else—and proceed to define it not by other op-
> erations than Thurstone's but by another series of noises, which have
> an expressive function comparable to exclamations of joy or sadness,
> laughter, or lyric poetry, but which have no objective representative
> function at all.[8]

To the extent that this statement means that we can never get away
from being explicit about our research procedures and measurement
descriptions, we do not object to it. But when operationalism is
construed to mean that anything social that can be recorded and
measured should command our attention as sociologists, then we object.
In terms of confirmation of theories, it is plain that only those indicators
that have counterparts in definitions of determinants and results are
worthwhile. When verifying a theory, other measurement devices may
very well be worthless and irrelevant.

The vindications for the use of conventional nominal definitions are
many. One is that they can enter into the logical relationships that make

---

[8] George A. Lundberg, *Foundations of Sociology*, (New York: The Macmillan
Company, 1939), p. 59. In his *Social Research* revised edition, (New York: Long-
mans, Green and Co., 1941), p. 7, Lundberg, however, advocates the same approach
to the relation between theorizing and research operations as we have done here.

the advantage of theory—particularly axiomatic theory—possible more readily than can operational definitions. If we accept the orthodox operationalism, we make it unduly difficult to obtain the advantages of theorizing. The insistence that all definitions should be operational also leads to other rather undesirable consequences. If fully accepted, it means that a change of operational definition implies a change in the proposition being tested. Also it would be impossible to disprove an earlier accepted proposition with new and better indicators.

One may question, on this occasion, the place of operationalism in sociology. A very legitimate aspect of operationalism concerns the definitions of score values on variables. When we are asked, not *what variable* a certain scale measures, but *what value* a certain score on this scale signifies, we give our answer in terms of a description of the scoring technique, the standardization group, etc., in short, an operational definition.[9]

Nothing said above should be construed as an appeal to keep definitions and indicators at arm's length. They should instead embrace each other in the most intimate way When we ask how "valid" the indicators are, we are asking about the intimacy of this embrace.

---

[9] *Cf.* Gösta Carlsson, *Dimensions of Behavior,* (Lund: C. W. K. Gleerup, 1949), ch. 2.

43

CHAPTER V

# ON THE DECISIONS IN VERIFICATIONAL STUDIES

In this chapter we propose to comment on the different decisions required in the enterprise of confirming a sociological proposition by research. We want to cover a large number of decisions in the research process, using only the briefest illustrations. Those who have not participated in social research or read textbooks about techniques of social research may want to read only the conclusions of this chapter.

INTERNAL VALIDITY

Validity, ecliptically speaking, is the extent to which an indicator corresponds to a definition. The question of validity thus goes to the core of the relation between theory and data. Part of Newton's genius is due to the fact that he could see that the indicators used in astronomy could be validly coordinated to definitions used to interpret data from small scale experiments. The progress toward validity lies in a continuous adjustment of theorizing to the techniques of research, and in a

44

continuous adjustment of techniques of research to theorizing. Unfortunately, contemporary sociologists sometimes seem to lack good understanding of the principle. New methods are often developed in a theoretical vacuum, sometimes in response to practical needs. And whole conceptual systems are published without the slightest hint as to how their concepts should be translated into research operations.

Guttman has divided the issue of validity into "internal" validity and "external validity.[1] The major difference is that the former expresses a "logical" relationship, while the latter expresses an "empirical relationship." Internal validity, in other words, can be appreciated without empirical studies, while the determination of external validity is a test of a hypothesis. Let us begin by discussing the former.

Perfect validity means that the indicator has the same scope of content as the definition. Some typical problems of internal validity might now be illustrated. Let us assume that our nominal definition is one of "work satisfaction." Let us represent it with a circle—

Let the indicators, *e.g.* a questionnaire to record work satisfaction, be represented by a broken circle—

[1] Louis Guttman, "The Problem of Attitude and Opinion Measurement," in Samuel Stouffer (ed.), *Measurement and Prediction*, (Princeton: Princeton University Press, 1950), pp. 57-59.

Or, more generally, the solid circle represents sentences that enter into the nominal definition, and the broken circle represents the sentences describing the indicators.

We may distinguish the following typical problems of validity.

(1) The definition implies the indicator and, in addition, something other than the indicator.

This would, for example, be the case if we had the response, "I am satisfied with the ventilation where I work" as the operational definition of work satisfaction. Obviously the term "work satisfaction" implies more than satisfaction with the ventilation.

(2) The indicator implies the definition and, in addition, something other than the definition:

This would, for example, be the case if we had the response, "I like it here in X-town" as the indicator of "work satisfaction."

(3) The indicator implies the definition and vice versa:

The response, "I like my friends and acquaintances here in X-town" would represent this situation if it were used as an operational definition of "work satisfaction." The satisfaction with the fellow workers would belong to "work satisfaction", while satisfaction with leisure-time friends would not.

These three kinds of errors of internal validity may account for some of the contradictory results we have sometimes found when similar studies have been done around the same topic. One usually tries to minimize the effects of these errors by combining many indicators into one index. Indexes are formed according to rules for combining indicators. For verification purposes, one should use rules of index-formation which maximize the likelihood that the index will record the determinant (or result, as the case may be) of a proposition and distribute the errors at random—that is, all other factors it records. An index thus tends to let errors among its component indicators cancel out. However, it is well worth remembering that one single valid indicator is worth more than an index made up of numerous indicators of low validity. And too often one reads research reports in which the author has allowed a bunch of less valid indicators to contaminate one really valid indicator by pooling them all into one and the same index.

In the last analysis, the validity of our indicators can be judged only in the context of success of a theory. The acceptance by the scientific community of a theory gives content to its definitions and meaning to its indicators, and makes it possible to speak of them as having a close correspondence.

Validity can be achieved not only by changing one's indicators but by changing one's definitions. This interplay between definitions and indicators can be illustrated by two typical "aha-experiences":

"This dimension which my theory said was one and the same is actually several distinct dimensions in my data." One might assume that Neal Gross and his co-workers had this experience when they studied the role of high school superintendent.[2] Sociological theory has long assumed the concept "concensus of role prescriptions," the idea that many person agree on what is expected by the occupant of a given position. The indicators used by Gross, however, showed that there is considerable difference between what a group of school superintendents

---

[2] Neal Gross, *et. al.*, *Explorations in Role Analysis*, (New York: John Wiley and Sons, 1958), ch. 7.

agree is their role and what members of school boards, etc., agree is their role. This difference in the data leads Professor Gross and his co-workers to reformulate the concept of consensus of role prescriptions into two concepts—"interposition consensus" and "intraposition consensus" —and to develop separate indexes for them.

"These dimensions which my theories said were several distinct ones are actually one and the same in my data." In a review of small groups research we were struck by a peculiar circumstance: the indicators that members of a group evaluate each other favorably is in one research tradition linked to the definition of "sociometric popularity", in another to the definition of "cohesiveness", in a third to a definition of "sentiment", and in a fourth school of thought it is linked to "morale". It is, therefore, possible to reduce these to one—namely, the "favored valuations from associates". Here, then, several indicators in the research literature could be validly coordinated to one definition rather than to several definitions.

## EXTERNAL VALIDITY

Let us now proceed to external validity. External validity becomes important whenever we want to use one indicator as an index or prognosis of another indicator. The most common case of this in sociology is when we use a verbal expression as an index to other behavior. When we ask people about their social participation, we would like to know how they actually participate, not what they tell about their participation. The validity of a social participation item in a questionnaire is limited by the extent to which our respondent tells the truth. This is the case with many other indicators too. The number of sociometric choices received is a valid index of popularity, provided the respondents have told the truth about who their friends are. Monthly earnings, the number of school years completed, are likewise valid indexes of income and education only to the extent that they are accurately reported.[3]

---

[3] This analysis is not possible when the expressions to be analyzed are statements that are neither true nor false. Indicators of attitudes, values, and role-prescriptions

48

Now we know that some data used in sociological studies probably are inaccurate. There are reasons to believe that births from certain areas are under-reported; there are suspicions that crime statistics from some countries are faked for political reasons, etc. We know that people often lie in response to our interviewers. In Elmira, New York, 9 per cent of the individuals who told the interviewers that they had voted had actually not done so, according to the records of the Election Board.[4] The same is the case in a survey I did in Uppsala, Sweden. Out of 19 persons who did not vote we found that 11 told the interviewers that they had voted. The point can be duplicated from other surveys.

In the example of the voting question we can check the validity, because we know of an external, quite valid and reliable, criterion. In most cases, however, we lack such a criterion. Exploring the latter, the Uppsala survey found the following responses to the following questions:

| | | |
|---|---|---|
| Do you have as good table manners when you are at home as when you are at other people's homes? | Yes | 98% |
| Do you ever think badly of your closest friends? | No | 91% |
| Are you always sincerely happy over your friends' successes? | Yes | 82% |
| Do you sometimes have sexual thoughts which you think are improper or immoral? | No | 79% |
| Do you always take time to listen to other people's problems? | Yes | 79% |

A psychologically sophisticated person is likely to believe that most of these responses are thoughtless untruths. It appears that most of the persons interviewed in this survey have responded in accordance with what they believe to be the standards of decent people. The majority refuse to admit that they have ever violated these standards. In short, they show a tendency toward conventionalized answers.

An assumed conventionality is, of course, only one of the many personality traits that render interpretations of statements about facts hazardous in surveys and historical documents. Other personality traits

belong, for example, here. Expressions like:
"I like X"
"X is good"
"Buy me X"
are, according to the philosophy we assume, neither empirically true nor empirically false. Accordingly, statements indicating attitudes, values, and norms are neither true nor false.

[4] Alice S. Kitt and David B. Gleichner, "Determinants of Voting Behavior", *Public Opinion Quarterly*, Vol. XVI (1950), p. 407.

may upset them in similar ways. The invalidity caused by convention-alized answers, however, seems to have traceable effects. Studies employing the interview method in the area of marital satisfaction are in amazing agreement with the conclusion that the person likely to love his wife also loved his parents, had a happy childhood, goes to church regularly, and, in number of ways, acts and feels according to what is considered to be virtuous. The hypothesis about a generalized tendency to conventionalize answers to interview questions makes these results less remarkable.

Lack of validity because of false information is, in principle, possible to detect. In practice, however, it is very troublesome, and we generally prefer to discover other facts than the extent to which informants lie. But, like the historians, we are obliged to check the truth of a piece of information before we use it. When the interview method is employed to obtain factual information, cross-checks can often be made. We can ask two respondents about the same facts. We can come back to the same respondent and ask him again. Such tests of agreement and consistency can never fully prove validity, but they can fully disprove validity.

RELIABILITY

Reliability is the extent to which an indicator renders unambiguous readings. Reliability is a necessary prerequisite for validity. Unreliable instruments always lack validity.

The current discussion of reliability lacks precision, a fact pointed out by Ekman.[5] Involved in the reliability term as used in psychology and sociology are at least four different measures:

1. The *congruency* of several indicators, that is, the extent to which several indicators measure the same thing.
2. The *precision* of an instrument (intra-individual reliability) that is, the extent to which the indicator registers in a consistent way for one observer.

_____

[5] Gösta Ekman, *Reliabilitet och konstans*, (Uppsala: Almqvist & Wiksell, 1947). Our definitions of the components of reliability differ somewhat from those given by Ekman. The differences are due to our desire to deal with the reliability of any indicator, not only psychological tests.

3. The *objectivity* of an instrument (inter-individual reliability), that is, the agreement of one scientist's reading of the indicator with the readings made by other scientists.

4. The *constancy* of an object measured, that is, the extent to which the object measured does not fluctuate.

One may conceive of the general method of separating these components as a complex analysis of variance according to a factorial design:

| *Time* | | $T_1$ | | | | $T_2$ | | | $T_3$ |
|---|---|---|---|---|---|---|---|---|---|
| *Observer* | A | B | C | | A | B | C | | |
| *Indicator* | 1 2 3 | 1 2 3 | 1 2 3 | ... | 1 2 3 | 1 2 3 | 1 2 3 | ... | ... |
| | x x x | x x x | x x x | ... | x x x | x x x | x x x | ... | ... |
| *Reading* | x x x | x x x | x x x | ... | x x x | x x x | x x x | ... | ... |
| | x x x | x x x | x x x | ... | x x x | x x x | x x x | ... | ... |

The variance between indicators reveals congruency; the variance between readings indicates precision; the variance between observers indicates objectivity; the variance between different times indicates constancy. There will remain the possibility of a residual error, represented by the different interaction effects.

No one has ever—to my knowledge—carried out this complex design and received estimates for all these types of errors of measurement. (The calculations, however, are not overly difficult, and this could be done.) However, we have many studies that include estimates of some of these sources of error and estimates of the total magnitude of measurement error. The cumulative experience of these studies has taught us to have confidence in certain measurement techniques, particularly those used in surveys and quantitative content analysis. Persons using these techniques, therefore, no longer feel obliged to go through the

51

tedious process of checking their reliability. But whenever a novel research technique emerges, the question of reliability becomes very pertinent. When sociological research uses sources and methods of historical research, possibilities for quantitative estimates of reliability become rare, perhaps non-existent. Historians have developed a special sense for these problems which, however, seems largely uncodified, so that it has to be learned in apprenticeships with established historians. Since sociological problems often call for historical data, efforts should be encouraged to make explicit the rules for evaluating the reliability of historical indicators.

The role of measurements in the development of theoretical sociology should not be exaggerated. Comparatively few theoretical advances in other sciences seem to have been inspired by refined measurement techniques, and I cannot think of any existing sociological proposition that owes its existence and plausibility primarily to a careful control of the errors of measurement.

SCOPE

By "scope" I mean the proportion of all possible sources of data which is represented in a given research.

A favorite example of the importance of scope is found in the generalization, "All swans are white". This was held true until Australia was discovered and her black swans became known. Social science knows of similar occurrences. Freud, developing his theory of the Oedipus complex, worked with cases from a population of rather authoritarian Viennese families. When the cultural anthropologists discovered a society in which a man lives in the home of his wife's parents, supports not by his own but his sister's children, behaves like a Western uncle toward his children while the children's uncle assumes the role of the father for his children, then there is no surprise in the fact that Freud's theory is not confirmed.[6] In both cases the theory could claim plausibility only in a limited population. When the scope was enlarged, the theory was disproved.

---

[6] Bronislaw Malinowski, *Sex and Repression in Savage Society*, (New York, The Humanities Press, 1927).

However, most theorizing claims universality. The universality of a sociological proposition is an assumption which we have to confirm by wide replications of our studies. When applicable, we have to confirm our propositions on different subject matters (political, religious, etc.) in different categories in the same society (professions, income brackets, educational levels, etc.) and in different societies (civilized and primitive, ancient and contemporary). This is an expensive process of demanding labor to be undertaken before we can claim a hypothesis to be truly verified.

Current practice nevertheless allows a great deal of extrapolation beyond the scope of our original data. In general, I regard these lax standards as reasonable. However, on two scores I have learned to be suspicious and suggest that an extrapolation should not be accepted in advance of proof. These are (1) generalizations from micro-sociology, *i.e.*, encounters, organizations, and markets, to macro-sociology, *i.e.*, institutional realms, systems of stratification, and culture; (2) generalizations from executive actions and realms, *i.e.*, economy, polity, and science, to emotive actions and realms, *i.e.*, art, religion, and ethics.

We may ask here what point there is in a single test of a hypothesis performed on a population with limited scope. If any bet has to be placed on the outcome of a test of the hypothesis outside this population, I think the following principle applies: "It is more probable that a hypothesis holds true outside the population on which it has been confirmed than that the contrary of the hypothesis holds true in the new population." It is hard to prove this point strictly—except, perhaps, through studies in the history of science—but I believe that this is a principle that we employ daily in common sense judgments. For example, when we stand in front of new doors, we treat the door handles according to this principle and turn them in the direction indicated by our experience with other door handles. In the long run, the principle seems to do more good than harm.

Furthermore, there is another important value in the test of a hypothesis on a population with limited scope. This, again, is an application of the rule that it is easier to prove a theory false than to prove it true. It is evident that to make a theory highly probable we have to show that it holds true in various populations. However, it is equally evident that to disprove a theory it is enough to demonstrate that it does

53

not hold true in one population, however limited in scope. To *disprove* is the primary task of the test performed with limited scope. If we fail in this attempt to disprove the proposition, we may start to think that it contains something valuable and go on to test with wider scope.

REPRESENTATIVENESS

Sociologists in general seem to have a very advanced conception of the role of samples in research. This sophistication has developed in descriptive sociology—not the sociology concerned with testing theories. Descriptive sociology has found it very convenient to describe a strictly defined universe through the use of various sampling techniques.

As is well known, we distinguish two kinds of samples in sociology: (1) probability samples, drawn by means of a randomizing device (*e.g.* tables of random numbers) and in which each subject in the population has a known or equal chance to get into the sample, and (2) judgment samples, in which we (or our interviewers) decide—at least within certain limits—who shall get into the sample and in which we have no exact knowledge that each subject in the population has a definite chance to get into the sample. In probability samples—simple ones and stratified ones—the probability of making a given error in generalizing the results from the sample to the universe from which the sample is drawn can be stated exactly. The judgment samples—for example, the quota samples—are not as good in this respect; there is no way of computing the probability of a certain error when we use them. However, they have found a pragmatic justification. (When George Gallup, at the time he used only judgment samples, said that his average error in presidential elections was 5 per cent, this is an indication of the degree of plausibility of the results from such samples). The procedures for statistical evaluations of the representative samples are well known, and there is no reason for entering into this topic. The question we have to answer is rather what importance we shall allocate to the representativeness of samples in the total verification process.

Consider again the universality of a theory. The relationships expressed in the theoretical propositions, in other words, claim to be universally present. They are, accordingly, present both in representative and non-representative samples. To disprove or demonstrate their existence is, hence, possible in any kind of sample—biased or unbiased. This important, and perhaps surprising, consideration, however, should immediately be qualified. When using a biased sample for a verification, we must have assurance that the relationship we want to prove is not introduced into our data by selective sampling. This possibility, however, is in most cases rather unlikely. Also, when using a biased sample for verification, we should realize that we have no knowledge of the population to which the result can be safely generalized. Furthermore, if the test of a given hypothesis involves, for example, mathematical constants computed on the basis of a representative sample, a biased sample might be avoided for further tests. This, however, is rarely the case in sociology. On balance, it appears that non-representative samples are not much inferior to representative samples when we want to disprove a theoretical hypothesis. This relatively minor importance of representativeness in verification studies is in sharp contrast to the overwhelming importance of representativeness of samples in descriptive studies.

Representativeness should not be confused with randomization. Randomization can be used to obtain representativeness. However, it is also used as a method of controlling irrelevant factors when testing a hypothesis. Randomization in the latter function is of the utmost importance, as will be shown next.

In summarizing, we may say that a large scope of the population on which a proposition is tested is necessary as a prerequisite for its acceptance. However, use of a population with a very limited scope is sufficient for the disproof of a theory. Representative samples from these populations are necessary if we want to know exactly how far we can safely generalize the result. However, they are of minor importance for the disproof of a theory and are not really an essential prerequisite for the acceptance of a theory. When the law of falling bodies was demonstrated by our physics teacher, he used various materials—stones, metals, wood, cloth and cotton—to show that they all fell equally fast in a room practically free from air. He did not take representative samples of all these materials but chose a wide scope for the population of material to be included—the scope ranging from metal to cotton. Galileo, who first proved the hypothesis, proceeded in the same way, disregarding representativeness in favor of the scope of the population. To our knowledge, he has never been blamed for this.

## DESIGNS

We use the word "design" to indicate the way we arrange to produce the readings of our indicators. Different designs give different plausibilities to a test of a proposition, and we must learn to evaluate designs.

As mentioned, we can never prove a proposition in any strict sense. The best piece of proof we have is that our proposition can predict observations. This is an incomplete proof, since we always run the risk that new observations will disqualify our prediction or that alternative propositions will predict observations equally well. However, we can with the greatest certainty disprove our proposition. A conventional test of a proposition is to disprove its opposite, the null-hypothesis. The outcome should be based on: (a) the extent to which our data fall in the direction predicted by the hypothesis; (b) the certainty with which we have disproved the null-hypothesis; and (c) the certainty and extent to which we have disproved alternative hypotheses to the working hypothesis. Designs might be evaluated in these three respects.

It is common to distinguish between *cross-sectional* and *longitudinal* designs for tests of hypotheses. In sociology they are represented by, for example, the survey method and the panel technique, respectively. Suppose that $x$ is the determinant and $y$ the result. In a cross-sectional design we measure a sample of $n$ units, at the time $t_1$ with regard to $x$ and $y$. The data we obtain consists of two series such as the following:

$$
\begin{array}{cc}
{}^{t_1}X_1 & {}^{t_2}Y_1 \\
{}^{t_1}X_2 & {}^{t_2}Y_2 \\
{}^{t_1}X_3 & {}^{t_2}Y_3 \\
| & | \\
{}^{t_1}X_n & {}^{t_2}Y_n
\end{array}
$$

In the longitudinal design, we measure a sample of $n$ individuals at the times $t_1$, $t_2$, $t_3$, etc., with regard to $x$ and $y$. The data we have are series like the following:

$$t_1 X_1 \qquad t_1 Y_1 \qquad\qquad t_2 X_1 \qquad t_2 Y_1$$
$$t_1 X_2 \qquad t_1 Y_2 \qquad\qquad t_2 X_2 \qquad t_2 Y_2$$
$$t_1 X_3 \qquad t_1 Y_3 \qquad\qquad t_2 X_3 \qquad t_2 Y_3$$
$$t_1 X_4 \qquad t_1 Y_4 \qquad\qquad t_2 X_4 \qquad t_2 Y_4$$

$$t_1 X_n \qquad t_1 Y_n \qquad\qquad t_2 X_n \qquad t_2 Y_n$$

It can be demonstrated that the longitudinal design is more effective than the cross-sectional. This is shown in various ways. If we are concerned with disproving the hypothesis that $x$ is the cause of $y$ on a common sense level, the demonstration of the superiority of the longitudinal design could be carried out like this. In the cross-sectional design we should order the individuals according to their values of $x$. If the hypothesis is correct, the values of $y$ should follow the same order after this procedure. In the longitudinal design we may first carry out the very same test as the one in the cross-sectional design. However, in addition to this, we can perform a second test. We can compare the individuals with regard to $x$ at the two different times, $t_1$ and $t_2$. If we

57

arrange them in proportion to the extent they gained or lost in $x$ between $t_1$ and $t_2$, the hypothesis states that their gains or losses in $y$ should follow the same order. It should be realized that the latter test is different from the former. It is conceivable that the first test in the longitudinal design may make us accept the hypothesis while the latter test rejects the hypothesis. Since the first test is the one employed in the straight cross-sectional design, we conclude that longitudinal designs are more sensitive than cross-sectional designs. The former stand a better chance of disproving the working hypothesis. The latter, however, are by far more common in sociology.

Longitudinal designs can be further sub-divided into *retrospective* and *prospective* designs. These designs represent two somewhat different ways of performing a test about determinant and result. We may observe what our proposition has called the result and then inquire as to whether it was preceded by the hypothesized determinant. Let us call this procedure, which advances from the establishment of effects to the establishment of causes, the retrospective design. On the other hand, we can observe what our proposition terms the determinant and then investigate whether it is followed by the hypothesized result. This procedure, which goes from the establishment of causes to the establishment of effects, we may term the prospective design.

In order to evaluate the restrospective and the prospective design, let us again assume that we have the hypothesis, "$x$ is a determinant of $y$." If all cases in our population have both the properties X and Y,

$$X_1 - Y_1$$
$$X_2 - Y_2$$
$$X_3 - Y_3$$
$$| \quad |$$
$$| \quad |$$
$$| \quad |$$
$$X_n - Y_n$$

it is plain that both the retrospective and prospective design would confirm the hypothesis. Suppose, however, that some of the cases fail to show the property Y, and let us indicate such a case by writing X-O:

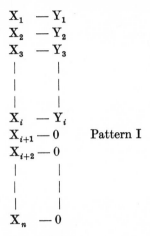

$$X_1 \;-\; Y_1$$
$$X_2 \;-\; Y_2$$
$$X_3 \;-\; Y_3$$
$$X_i \;-\; Y_i$$
$$X_{i+1} \;-\; 0 \qquad \text{Pattern I}$$
$$X_{i+2} \;-\; 0$$
$$X_n \;-\; 0$$

If our data show this pattern, the retrospective design would make us accept the hypothesis, since Y is always preceded by X. However, using the prospective design on this pattern of data, we reject the hypothesis, since all X are not alwayys followed by Y.

The case is reversed when some of our cases fail to show the property X:

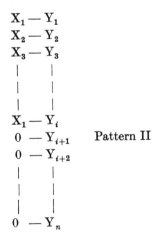

$$X_1 - Y_1$$
$$X_2 - Y_2$$
$$X_3 - Y_3$$
$$X_1 - Y_i$$
$$0 \;-\; Y_{i+1} \qquad \text{Pattern II}$$
$$0 \;-\; Y_{i+2}$$
$$0 \;-\; Y_n$$

Using the retrospective design on this pattern of data, we would reject the hypothesis, since all Y are not preceded by X. The prospective design, however, would make us accept the hypothesis, since all X are followed by Y.

These peculiarities become important for research evaluations once we realize what kind of causal relationships these patterns allow us to assume. In Pattern I we are free to assume that *x* is a necessary and contingent cause of *y*. In other words, *x* is essential, but so are other factors in order to produce *y*. The retrospective design is, then, adequate in making us accept the hypothesis about a necessary but not sufficient cause.

In Pattern II we are free to assume that *x* is a sufficient and substitutable cause of *y*. In other words, it is true that *y* is a result of *x* and that *y* may also be produced by other factors than *x*. The prospective design, then, is adequate in making us accept the hypothesis about a sufficient but not necessary cause. When a hypothesis is accepted by the retrospective design and accepted by the prospective design, we may deal with a sufficient but not necessary cause. When both designs make us accept the hypothesis, we may have a necessary and sufficient cause.

Up to this point we have dealt only with verification in terms of rejection of a hypothesis contrary to the working hypothesis. Let us move to the further criterion of verification in terms of rejection of alternative hypotheses.

The problem of the ruling out of alternative hypotheses is known as the problem of "control" in a verification enterprise. We should distinguish between the control of known alternative hypotheses and the control of unknown alternative hypotheses. The best method of verification controls both known and unknown alternatives. A method of this extraordinary kind does exist and is known as the *experimental* design.

The experimental design controls alternatives by producing the hypothesized determinant and by randomization of known and unknown factors. The experimenter does not merely observe what his hypothesis assumes as the determinant, but, in addition, himself produces it. In an effort to obtain a base line for measuring the possible effect, he would use a minimum of two groups in his experiment, one in which the determinant is produced—the experimental group—and one in which nothing is done—the control group. In order further to control the in-

Designs

fluence of alternative hypotheses, he assigns subjects at random to the experimental group and the control group. By so doing, he obtains maximum likelihood that the groups are similar in all respects except one: the produced determinant in the experimental group. Accordingly, he is reasonably confident that any difference between the control group and the experimental group is due to the introduced determinant.

Experimental designs may be longitudinal, involving repeated measurement of the same subjects. These and other more effective designs have developed in close connection with the statistical techniques going along with analyses of the results—notably, analysis of variance. The latter has also provided the possibility of testing several hypotheses in the same experimental design.

The advantages of the experimental design, however, rest with the possibility of a random assignment of cases to the experimental and control groups and on the possibility of producing what the working hypothesis terms the cause. Unfortunately, in sociology we rarely have these possibilities.

Certainly many factors are intentionally introduced into a society by politicians, educators, welfare agencies, etc. But these phenomena are seldom or never produced, because they are termed causes in a scientific social theory. Furthermore, when compulsory education, socialized medicine, public housing projects, etc., are introduced into a society, the very complexity of the new phenomena does not make them suitable as indicators of concepts of a theory.

In the second place, we can rarely introduce randomization of the persons supposed to enjoy these intentionally produced phenomena without violating strong moral sentiments. As to the social programs of the welfare state Chapin makes the comment:

> The conventional method of equalizing factors that are known and also unknown (by R. A. Fisher's design of experiment) is to select at random both the experimental group that receives treatment and the control group that serves as a reference group for comparison. In social research the program of social treatment cannot be directed toward a randomly selected group because the prevailing mores require that this treatment be directed to a group of individuals who are eligible because of greater *need*. Thus precise control of unknown is impossible and the only factors that can be controlled are

61

factors that are known to be in the particular social situation because of previous studies.[7]

It seems that this inability to satisfy the conditions for a profitable use of the experimental design would definitely curtail the sociologist's prospect to verify his theories. However, the situation is by no means disastrous: sciences like meteorology and astronomy have verified theories without the employment of the experimental method.

For control of alternative hypotheses, the sociologist is to a large extent dependent on what might be called *pseudo-experimental* designs. These designs control propositions known as alternative ones, but, unlike the experimental designs, these designs cannot control unknown alternatives.

The most commonly used method in sociology for control of known alternative propositions is multivariate analysis, which has been formalized by Paul Lazarsfeld.[8] Skill in its use has become essential for most sociological research; those who know how to use it deserve to be called "modern sociologists". The technique controls alternative propositions by testing the hypothesis in sub-samples that are homogeneous with respect to the determinants specified by the alternative propositions. It can be used to control all known alternative determinants, provided the sample used is large enough.

The simplest relation between two variates $x$ and $y$ is a four-fold table:

|        | X | non-X |   |
|--------|---|-------|---|
| Y      |   |       |   |
| non-Y  |   |       |   |

---

[7] F. Stuart Chapin, "Experimental Designs in Social Research", *American Journal of Sociology*, Vol. LV (1950), p. 402. (Italics in the original).

[8] Paul F. Lazarsfeld, "Interpretation of Statistical Relations as a Research Operation" in Paul F. Lazarsfeld and Morris Rosenberg (ed.), *The Language of Social Research*, (Glencoe, Ill.: The Free Press, 1955), pp. 115-125.

To discover whether a third variable, $z$, accounts for any of the relations found in such a table, we break it into two parts:

|        | X | non-X |
|--------|---|-------|
| Y      |   |       |
| non-Y  |   |       |

=

|  Z     | X | non-X |
|--------|---|-------|
| Y      |   |       |
| non-Y  |   |       |

+

| non-Z  | X | non-X |
|--------|---|-------|
| Y      |   |       |
| non-Y  |   |       |

If the relation between $x$ and $y$ still holds in all sub-classes of $z$, we may retain, for the time being, our trust in the proposition that $x$ affects $y$. To this kind of design many new alternative determinants can be added, and it works equally well for qualitative and quantitative varieties.

However, the advantages do not end here. We can tabulate:

|        | X | non-X |
|--------|---|-------|
| Z      |   |       |
| non-Z  |   |       |

=

|   Y    | X | non-X |
|--------|---|-------|
| Z      |   |       |
| non-Z  |   |       |

+

| non-Y  | X | non-X |
|--------|---|-------|
| Z      |   |       |
| non-Z  |   |       |

and also:

|  | Y | non-Y |  |  | Y | non-Y |  |  | Y | non-Y |  |
|---|---|---|---|---|---|---|---|---|---|---|---|
| Z |  |  |  | Z |  |  |  | Z |  |  |  |
|  |  |  | = |  |  |  | + |  |  |  |  |
| non-Z |  |  |  | non-Z |  |  |  | non-Z |  |  |  |

(with column headings **X** over the middle block and **non-X** over the right block)

The purpose of these tabulations is to discover the actual linkage between the three variables. It would carry us far to review all the rules of interpretation involved here. However, if certain assumptions about the time lag between the variates can be made, it is possible to use such tabulations to disentangle a wide variety of causal chains, as shown in the adjoining diagram adapted from Dahlström:[9]

Another method of pseudo-experimental control is that of *matching*, advocated by F. S. Chapin.[10] An experimental group and a control group are made equal on some criteria by discarding cases in one group for which no "twin" can be found in the other group. One disadvantage of this procedure is that the matched groups so obtained are not representative of the original groups. When this way of matching is employed, we do not quite know to what population the results can be generalized.

Control in pseudo-experimental design can be obtained through the use of other statistical adjustments. Various applications of the *multiple regression* approach can be made, provided variables fitting

---

[9] Edmund Dahlström, "Analys av surveymaterial" in Georg Karlsson, *et al.*, (eds.), *Sociologiska metoder*, (Stockholm: Svenska Bokförlaget, 1961), p. 193.

[10] F. Stuart Chapin, *Experimental Designs in Sociological Research*, (New York: Harper and Brothers, 1947).

(1)  X → Y → Z         (2)  X → Z → Y

(3)  Z → X → Y         (4)  X
                            ↘
                             Y
                            ↗
                         Z

(5)  X              (6)  X              (7)  X
     ↑↘                  ↓↘                  ↑↘
     ↓ Y                   Y                   Y
     Z↗                  Z↗                  Z↗

(8)  X              (9)  X              (10)  X
     ↑                   ↑↘                   ↑
     ↓ Y                 ↓ Y                  ↓ Y
     Z↗                  Z                    Z↗

(11)  X             (12)  X             (13)  X
      ↓↘                  ↓                   ↑
        Y                   Y                 ↓ Y
      Z                   Z↗                  Z↙↗

the rather rigid assumptions are used. The most common methods are
those of partial correlation and analysis of covariance. These methods
become rather laborious if the number of factors to be controlled is
more than three or four.

Experimental designs and pseudo-experimental designs may be cross-
sectional or longitudinal. We have already pointed out that longitudinal designs are more effective than cross-sectional designs and that
experimental designs are more effective than pseudo-experimental designs. We can now reach a typology of designs:

65

*On the Decisions in Verificational Studies*

| | | The test of the null-hypothesis | |
|---|---|---|---|
| | | Cross-sectional | Longitudinal |
| The control of alterna- tive hypo- theses | No control | | |
| | Pseudo-experimental | | |
| | Experimental | | |

The closer a design comes to the longitudinal experimental the better it is. However, we know little or nothing about how to evaluate cross-wise combinations of the two criteria. We have no way in which to tell whether a pseudo-experimental longitudinal design (such as a panel with multi-variable analysis) is as effective as the cross-sectional experimental design (the conventional laboratory experiment).

Most quantitative sociological research—particularly public opinion polling—is cross-sectional without controls. Most non-quantitative sociological research—the case studies, for example—is longitudinal without controls. A superior user of the survey method introduces pseudo-experimental controls in his designs; perhaps he makes repeated interviews with the same group, thus rendering his design longitudinal in addition. This is about as far as field studies can ever reach in precision. A person using non-quantitative methods can also use pseudo-experimental controls. Max Weber attempted to find situations in the history of Asia which resembled the situation in urban Europe after the Reformation, with the exception of the religious factor present in Europe.[11] His findings became additional evidence for his hypothesis that Protestantism played a role in the creation of capitalism. Such a design should count upon a fair plausibility.

A limited range of problems of sociology is open to the experimental design. The results from methodologically adequate experiments in group dynamics should be viewed as highly plausible, and ingenuity should be encouraged when bringing problems into the laboratory. Since symbolic interaction is a major realm of sociological study and language variables are easily taken into the laboratory, it should be possible to

---

[11] For a brief summary of the variables that enter into Max Weber's comparative studies of world religions, see Reinhard Bendix, *Max Weber: An Intellectual Portrait*, (Garden City, N. Y.: Doubleday, 1960), ch. 8.

use experimental design to a greater extent than is now the case. The very fact that laboratory experiments have the higher verificational power is, however, no sufficient reason immediately to bring all research problems to the laboratory. Lippitt thinks that it is often most strategic to start with a survey about a problem, go on to a field experiment, and then subject the problem to a laboratory experiment.[12]

There is a strong movement towards quantification and statistical analysis in sociology. It should be noted, however, that the use of statistics is no substitute for theorizing. Churchman concludes as follows concerning the proper place of statistics:

> One cannot simply take a set of data, make certain distribution hypotheses about their populations, and proceed to a statistical test; one cannot do so and expect a meaningful answer will be the result. To paraphrase Kant, statistical tests without theory are blind: no general results can be asserted, no predictions made unless one assumes that the statistical hypotheses are consequences of a general theory within which prediction can be made independent of specialized restrictions. . . . We may therefore take the following to be the criterion for the meaningfulness of statistical tests: *every statistical hypothesis should be a consequence of a formal theory of nature.*[13]

Nor do we believe that statistics is the only acceptable method of evaluating a test of a proposition. As has been suggested above, non-quantitative methods, under certain circumstances, give equally plausible or more plausible results than some quantitative methods. The main reason for the use of quantitative variables treated statistically is that we obtain through them a quantitative expression of the plausibility of the null-hypothesis. As is well known, we must be aware of two kinds of error in testing a null-hypothesis:

> Errors of Type I: The null-hypothesis is actually true, but we reject it on the basis of our test. In other words, a false hypothesis is accepted.

12 Ronald Lippitt, "The Strategy of Socio-Psychological Research" in James G. Miller (ed.), *Experiments in Social Process,* (New York: McGraw-Hill Book Company, 1950), pp. 17-30. *Cf.* Leon Festinger, "Laboratory Experiments: The Role of Group Belongingness",*ibid.,* p. 33.

13 C. West Churchman, *Theory of Experimental Inference,* (New York, The Macmillan Company, 1948), p. 218. (Italics in the original).

Errors of Type II: The null-hypothesis is actually false, but we accept it on the basis of our test. In other words, a true hypothesis is rejected.

The use of statistical significance tests renders a measure, expressed as a level of probability, which can be used in evaluating the risk of making errors of Type I. Not so that this significance level *is* the probability of making errors of Type I, but by consistently applying a given significance level, such as the .05 level, we know that in the long run we have rejected only 5 per cent of the true null-hypotheses.

Thus, the use of quantification and statistics renders a standard for judging the null-hypothesis. As to the control of the alternative hypothesis, we have already noted that the statistical technique of randomization provides the most powerful control and that other techniques, such as multivariate analysis, also provide useful controls. Finally, quantification provides the most precise appreciation of the criteria for accepting a proposition which we have not yet discussed: the extent to which the data fall in the direction predicted by the hypothesis.

A favorite illustration of the latter is the confirmation of the hypothesis that an additional planet, Neptune, exists. When the motions of the planet Uranus were studied, a discrepancy was found between the actual orbit and the orbit predicted by Newton's law of gravitation. The discrepancy could be explained by hypothesizing an additional planet at a certain position. Eventually a planet, Neptune, was discovered in the vicinity of this predicted position. We realize that this was possible through the existence of very precise propositions phrased in quantitative variables. A sociological illustration of the same process of verification has been given by Coleman.[14]

We may hypothesize that the flow of scientific information among physicians is due to the fact that they talk with each other and pass on new information in personal communication. Assuming that each physician has an equal probability of communicating an item to the others per time unit, we can then express the rate of diffusion of information about, say, a new drug by a "logistic" formula:

$$X_{t+1} = X_t + k_1 X (1-X) \tag{1}$$

---

[14] James C. Coleman, Elihu Katz and Herbert Menzel, "The Diffusion of Innovation Among Physicians", *Sociometry*, vol. 20 (1957), pp. 253-270. A fuller report is contained in a forthcoming book by the same authors.

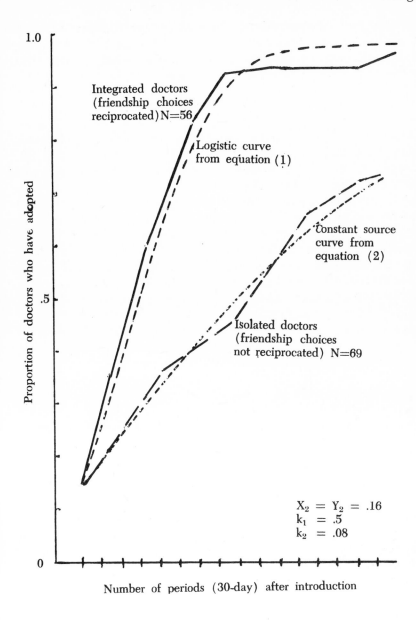

Integrated doctors
(friendship choices
reciprocated) N=56

Logistic curve
from equation (1)

Constant source
curve from
equation (2)

Isolated doctors
(friendship choices
not reciprocated) N=69

$X_2 = Y_2 = .16$
$k_1 = .5$
$k_2 = .08$

Proportion of doctors who have adopted

1.0

.5

0

Number of periods (30-day) after introduction

## On the Decisions in Verificational Studies

An alternative proposition is that information about the new drug, like a pure advertising campaign, reaches a fixed number of persons per time unit, independent of the number who have already learned about it. We then obtain a "constant source" formula:

$$Y_{t+1} = Y_t + k_2(1-Y) \tag{2}$$

In this case, our propositions make rather specific predictions, and a good quantitative measure can be obtained for the dependent variable. The theory says that the logistic pattern will prevail when doctors associate with each other and that the more linear pattern will predominate when they are isolated from each other. Sociometric questions about friends can be used to separate the integrated from the isolated doctors. Their respective rates of adoption of the drug tetracycline is shown in the chart above, together with the rates predicted fro mthe theory. We see that the predictions are reasonably close to the data. When complex predictions of this kind turn out correctly, one is tempted to accept the theory without further controls.

### THE COMPOSITE JUDGMENT OF ACCEPTANCE OR REJECTION

We have now completed our discussion of some of the various components of a decision to accept or reject a proposition in sociological research. In looking back at the complexities of evaluating internal and external validity of the indicators, their precision and objectivity, the representativeness of the sample, the scope of the data, the control of alternative hypotheses, the fit between predictions and observations, etc., one conclusion stands out: No presently known mechanical or mathematical device can help the sociologist in his decision to accept or reject a proposition, only good training and much expereince.

70

How stiff should our criteria be? The ideal of science prescribes standards that few, if any, concrete research projects ever meet. The surest way of damning any research report is to compare it with the ideals of science. The best way of evaluating a research report is to compare it with other research reports, the most reputable ones in our field. Looking at the most reputable specimens of sociological research, we find, not unexpectedly, that standards vary from place to place, from time to time, from topic to topic. What is acceptable at Columbia University may be unacceptable at Stockholm University; what was acceptable in the 1930's is unacceptable in the 1960's; what is acceptable in macro-sociology is unacceptable in micro-sociology. To test satisfactorily a single given proposition by means of a sociological research project is clearly extraordinarily difficult. To a considerable extent, sociological research is the art of the possible and must be judged accordingly.

# CHAPTER VI

# THE CONFIRMATION OF COMPLEX THEORIES

As we have seen, the confirmation of a proposition is a complex and rather tedious enterprise. Since the proofs are so long while life is so short, it is essential to devote our research efforts to hypotheses that are strategic. Some of the more sophisticated ways of ordering our propositions can aid us in selecting the most strategic ones and guide us in the expenditure of research efforts. It sounds paradoxical, but it is actually easier to test systems of propositions, *i.e.* theories, than single propositions.

This holds primarily for theories organized as matrixes, chains, or axiomatic systems. But such simple modes of ordering propositions as inventories of determinants and results also aid the strategy of research. Such inventories give us listings of factors to include in an empirical study. It is important to make sure that the recurrent variable—the result in the case of inventories of determinants, and the determinant in the case of inventories of results—is given the best possible measurement and that special research efforts are made in constructing its indicator. The reason for this is simple: this variable occurs in all tests, and if it is faulty the entire research effort is wasted.

Using the more sophisticated ways of ordering propositions, we employ the strategic principle of testing those propositions that have the greatest pay-off value in the form of deduced additional propositions. However, in any concrete instance, we will probably work with theories in which some of the propositions are already adequately supported by data. Here we may proceed differently. First, we assess the amount of support that past research gives to each proposition. Second, we make selections of unsupported propositions that, in combination with each other and with supported propositions, can derive the largest number of unsupported propositions. The shortest selection then becomes the one with the highest research priority. However, the shortest selection may not contain propositions that are easily subject to test, and we may for practical reasons consider some of the longer selections. In short, we make compromises between the difficulty of testing a proposition and its deductive power. In this way we get the most out of our research effort, the most in the form of direct or deduced support to previously unsupported propositions in our theory. In no instance should we have to test every proposition in a well organized theory.

Let us review some of the interplay between the ordering of propositions and the efforts of research. We may use an axiomatic theory as our example, since an axiomatic theory best illustrates the advantages we can obtain from theorizing when doing research.

## AXIOMATIC THEORIES AND RESEARCH

We have earlier illustrated some modes of axiomatic theories. We already know that this type of ordering of propositions serves the theorist in one essential way: it spells out all propositions implicit in some propositions. Now let us see how it serves the researcher.

Let us assume that we have reviewed or conducted research on a number of social groups with respect to (a) the number of associates per member in the group; (b) the solidarity of the group; (c) the consensus of the beliefs, values, and norms in the group; (d) the division of labor in the group; and (e) the extent to which persons are rejected (excluded) from the group when they violate group norms. Assume that these variables were found to be related in the following way:

73

1. The greater the division of labor, the greater the consensus.
2. The greater the solidarity, the greater the number of associates per member.
3. The greater the number of associates per member, the greater the consensus.
4. The greater the consensus, the smaller the number of rejections of deviants.
5. The greater the division of labor, the smaller the number of rejections of deviants.
6. The greater the number of associates per member, the smaller the number of rejections of deviants.
7. The greater the division of labor, the greater the solidarity.
8. The greater the solidarity, the greater the consensus.
9. The greater the number of associates per member, the greater the division of labor.
10. The greater the solidarity, the smaller the number of rejections of deviants.

If these relations appear in our research as simple correlations, we can only assume that the linkage between determinant and result in these propositions is stochastic and reversible.

These propositions can be ordered axiomatically in a variety of ways. If we select as postulates the last four findings, we obtain a somewhat distorted version of Durkheim's theory of division of labor.[1] Let us restate them with roman numbers:

I. The greater the division of labor, the greater the solidarity.
II. The greater the solidarity, the greater the consensus.
III. The greater the number of associates per member, the greater greater the division of labor.
IV. The greater the solidarity, the smaller the number of rejections of deviants.

These four propositions can be used to devise the other findings which thus become theorems. I and II render (1); I and III render (2). II and (2) render (3); II and IV render (4). I and IV render (5), and III and (5) render (6). The ten findings were reduced to four.[2]

---

[1] Emile Durkheim, *De la Division du travail social*, Paris, Felic, Alcan, 1893, (English edition available from The Free Press, New York). It should perhaps be stressed that nothing in this chapter is intended as a review or criticism of this classical work.

[2] We ignore the complications posed by the task to reduce also the number of reversible propositions.

This illustrates the *first* virtue of theorizing for the researcher: a theory can be used to provide the most parsimonious summary of actual or anticipated research findings.

Suppose now that we did not ourselves conduct all the ten studies that resulted in our findings. We have instead ten different researchers who do not know of one another and who, independent of one another, confirm one each of the ten propositions. On the basis of their investigation, they have some but not much confidence in their findings. They know how hard it is to confirm a single proposition. Let us, for the sake of argument, say that this confidence can be represented by a probability of .85; they and their colleagues judge that there are about 85 chances out of 100 that they have really hit upon something true.

Suppose further that we have a more theoretically oriented sociologist, who formulates a theory like the one above, and that he has performed exactly the same tests as our ten researchers, and that he, too, assigns a plausibility of .85 that each single test supports its hypothesis. However, when this theorist now talks of any of the ten propositions he can claim that their plausibility goes way beyond .85.

The reason for this claimed gain in probability is that the scientist working with theory—although he performs the same test as the scientist without a theory—also verifies several implications of his hypothesis. His procedure is practically identical with replications of a statistical test. The evidence from the tests of the implications reflects on the hypotheses as additional support according to a well known law of probability calculus.

This virtue of the axiomatic theory can be used also in another way. Suppose our theoretically oriented researcher is satisfied with a probability of .95. To obtain this he may verify only a selection of hypotheses—for example, the first five or six in our list. If he establishes them with a probability of .95, he can claim that his whole theory has about the same probability. Through the use of his theory he has saved a great deal of experimental work. The amount of probability transferred is a matter of some debate. Most writers hold that a deduction carries the same probability as the proposition from which it is deduced. However, in sociology we should not claim too much from the transfer of probability, since our deductions are not too precise, so long as our concepts are defined in normal prose and the deduction rules of ordinary language are used.

Thus we claim as the *second* and cardinal virtue of theorizing for the researcher that a theory can be used to coordinate research so that many separate findings support each other, giving the highest plausibility to the theory per finding.

Here, then, is the explanation of why it is comparatively hard to confirm a proposition but comparatively easy to confirm a theory. We can readily give modest empirical support to any of our propositions, but this is usually not enough to have much confidence in any one, if taken by itself. But a theory can coordinate these modest supports into high support for its postulates.

A further advantage of a theory is that we can, at any stage of the the verification enterprise, figure out what parts of the theory are confirmed and what parts remain as uncertain hypotheses. This is particularly useful when we want to economize our research efforts by locating research topics which will contribute most to the confirmation of a theory.

Using the same example as before, assume that we want to test whether division of labor leads to greater solidarity. Assume further that we do not have indicators of division of labor and solidarity for the same collectivities, nor can we conceive of any within the limits of our research budget. We have, however, informal or formal observations indicating that greater solidarity results in few outright rejections of deviants. Our reasoning is, then, the following. We want to test by implication:

I. The greater the division of labor, the greater the solidarity.

We may assume:

IV. The greater the solidarity, the smaller the number of rejections of deviates.

Hence we need to test:

5. The greater the division of labor, the smaller the number of rejections of deviates.

We find, thus, that we can test the latter hypothesis in order to give support to our postulate that division of labor leads to solidarity. The hypothesis thus selected is easier to test. We can easily coordinate its determinant and result to available indicators: for example, the division of labor may be indicated by the number of occupations in a society, and the number of rejections of deviants is indicated by the statistics on the persons executed, exiled, or locked up in correctional institutions for a longer time.

Thus we find a *third* virtue in theorizing for the researcher: a theory can be used to locate the most strategic or manageable propositions for testing.

Finally, let us consider an instance when our research fails to support a proposition which is part of a theory. Let us assume, for example, that research proves theorems (1), (2), and (3) but conclusively fails to support our proposition (5), that: The greater the division of labor, the smaller the number of rejections of deviants. Apparently, something must now be wrong with our theory, and the question arises which parts of the theory would now have to be rejected. We find this by deriving our postulates from our theorems, including the theorem that was proven wrong. We note that the false theorem was derived from Postulates I and IV. Hence either, or both, of these are false. However, as mentioned, we have good evidence for theorems (1), (2), and (3). Consider first (1) and (3).

> The greater the division of labor, the greater the consensus.
> The greater the number of associates per member, the greater the consensus.

Hence we obtain:

> The greater the division of labor, the greater the number of associates per member;

which, combined with (2) renders—

> The greater the solidarity, the greater the number of associates per member;

> The greater the division of labor, the greater the solidarity;

which is Postulate I. Thus our findings support Postulate I, and the falsehood is thus localized to Postulate IV. We must thus drop Postulate IV from our theory and also all theorems derived by means of Postulate IV—*i.e.*, theorems (4), (5), and (6). The rest of the theory is still tenable.

Here, then, is a *fourth* virtue of theory for the researcher: a theory provides a limited area in which to locate false propositions when a hypothesis fails to meet an empirical test.

*The Confirmation of Complex Theories*

To these four advantages could be added others. The ones we have reviewed seem to me to be most relevant for the present state of sociology. They are so important that no sociological researcher can afford to be ignorant of theory construction.

TESTING TOTAL THEORIES THROUGH THEIR CROSS PREDICTIONS

An impressive way of testing a theory is to use its component propositions to make one joint prediction and to demonstrate that this is an accurate prediction. Scientists in a hurry and with a flair for the spectacular have done this in several instances, and the theories so tested have become accepted by their colleagues. However convincing as this method may appear, it always contains elements of risk: several wrong premises may, of course, render the correct prediction. A critical colleague is never quite sure of the solidity of theories confirmed in this fashion. However, since we sociologists are in a hurry to deliver something else than promises and hopes to the society that supports us, a moderate encouragement of this procedure may be in order.

The joint predictions from several propositions can be arrived at through a careful use of theories phrased in ordinary language. Since deductions are sometimes complex, it may be most efficient to restate the propositions as mathematical equations and let the gross prediction be a solution to a series of equations. This is not because the mathematical language adds anything of substance to theoretical propositions; it does not. However, mathematical language has stricter rules for making derivations than the usual scholarly prose, and the derivations needed for gross predictions may be complex and in need of this extra precision.

Another way of making gross predictions is the use of allegories. These allegories, or *simulations,* as they are often called, are either verbal, mechanical, or electronic. A "utopia" is a verbal allegory. The "census clock" in the lobby of the Department of Commerce, Washington, D.C., is a well-known mechanical allegory which predicts the size of the population of the United States at any given time. It is a machine analogous to the simple proposition that any change in the size of population depends on a change in the number of births and deaths and/or the

78

number of immigrants and emigrants. Each decennial census provides a check on the adequacy of this simulation. It has recently been found that electronic calculators can be wired to function as flexible allegories to social processes. So far, only a few electronic simulations have been tested as to their accuracy in gross predictions; however, the development in this field moves very fast and carries great promise.

We may illustrate simulation procedures by using a form of verbal allegory. Consider the following stochastic propositions relevant to voting behavior:

1. Members of a primary group (family, friendship clique, informal work group) tend to vote for the same party.
2. The higher the occupational stratum of the members of a primary group, the greater the likelihood that it will vote for a rightist (conservative) party.
3. The more a primary group takes on the style of life of an occupational stratum, the more likely is it to vote like other primary groups in this occupational stratum.
4. The higher the proportion of salaried or wage-earning (as opposed to self-employed) persons in an occupational stratum, the more likely are members in its primary groups to vote for a social welfare party.

Add to these the following findings:

5. At present, families in the higher occupational strata in western countries have fewer children than have families in the lower occupational strata.
6. At present, the proportion of people in all occupational strata in western countries who work for salary or wage is increasing, and the number of self-employed is correspondingly decreasing.

Can we test all these propositions in one master stroke by checking how well they can account for the outcome of elections? To do this, we need facts about location of primary groups in occupational classes, the style of life in these groups, the mobility between occupational classes, the trends away from self-employment, and information about differential fertility in these classes, and attitudes toward welfare policies among salaried and self-employed. All this makes a number of tables, which, however, happen to be available in a large Swedish study from 1954-55 (N=2554). Furthermore, we need to make some assumption of the time element in several of the above propositions. This is not readily available and must be subject to some guessing. Finally, we

The Confirmation of Complex Theories

need to know which parties are Leftists and Rightists and which parties are in favor of social welfare measures. An allegorical statement of the behavior of the electorate in Sweden may now read as follows:

The age group that during 1950-55 has seen their chidren move into voting age consists of 51% Leftists (Social Democrats and Communists) and 49% Rightists (Conservatives, Liberals, and Agrarians). To avoid speaking in percentages let us put it this way: We have 51 Leftist homes and 49 Rightist homes with children who become voters. Let us see what happens to them over the next four national elections.

During a few years, 54 children growing up in Leftist homes come of voting age. Fourteen of these children happen to acquire Rightist friends or workmates at an early age. Three of them cannot resist the attraction of these friends or workmates and convert to the bourgeois view before they cast their first ballot. Remaining are thus 51 who at their first election opportunity vote with the Leftists, their parents' party.

Fifteen of these advance to become white-collar workers or entrepreneurs or marry into this group. Nine of them keep their past style of life; for example, they do not acquire an automobile. Three of them nevertheless adopt Rightist party preferences. Remaining are 48.

The remaining six who become white-collar workers or entrepreneurs buy a car, drink wine instead of beer with their food now and then, and four of them become bourgeois also in political aspects. Remaining are 44. One dies. Remaining are 43. However, four were gained from other parties, so their final count becomes 47.

During the same time, the following happens in the 49 Rightist homes. One way of paying for their higher standard is to have fewer children than the Leftists. Only 48 grow into voting age in the bourgeois homes. Four of these children acquire Leftist friends or workmates, and one converts to the Left before his first election. 47 are left.

Ten fall below their parents' station. Of them, four fail in their studies or marry below their station, but they keep their style of life and enjoy a car. A woman converts, however, to the Leftists. Remaining are 46.

Six of the others move from their parents' middle or upper class into the working class; some abandon their family farm in the country and appear in the cities as workers or workers' wives. Their money does not allow a car. Two become Socialists. One dies, which leaves 4 for the Rightists. However, as mentioned, they gained ten from the Leftists' parties which gives them a final count of 53.

Not much seems to have changed, but the apparently calm elec-

80

toral surface conceals a great deal. In the beginning the forecast for the Socialists seemed good. The parental vote had been 51 for the Leftists against 49 for the Rightists. The Leftists had more children than the Rightists, and the children voted at their first election 52 against 49 for the Socialists. The difference could have been even greater. In the course of time, almost three times as many deserted the Leftists as the Rightists. Rightist politicians are thus more successful than Leftist politicians as political evangelists and get the upwardly mobile as converts in their nets. However, the Leftists keep afloat as more diligent midwives. The final score after 20 years becomes 47 against 53 in favor of the Rightists. During the years that this process has taken place, the socialist parties in this age cohort have declined from 52 to 47 and the bourgeois parties increased from 49 to 53.

So far, we have told this story assuming that the Rightist and the Leftist parties have identical policies about social welfare. This was true in 1952 and virtually true in 1956. Let us amend this now by admitting that the Leftists in 1958 and 1960 proposed more generous social benefits in the form of pensions than did the Rightists. This has consequences. In the course of every four-year period, one of our 20 families with a self-employed member of the middle class faces a major problem: the man gives up being on his own, sells his shop or farm, and starts working for someone else. This has the result that more people during the period here considered become concerned over their pensions and get attracted to the welfare program of the Leftists. Half of these, or 2 persons, get to the point of voting for the Leftists. Furthermore, this greater generosity of the Leftists makes it a little harder to get converts from them among the upwardly mobile. Only 5 are gained for the Rightists instead of 10, as before. And it becomes easier for the Leftists to gain converts; 5 are gained instead of 4 before. All this changes the balance of our age cohort:

|  | *In 1968 if parties have identical welfare program* | *In 1968 if Leftists have more generous Pension program* |
|---|---|---|
| Rightists | 53 | 48 |
| Leftists | 47 | 52 |

In 1968, the all-important majority is solidly among the Leftists. The difference introduced by the different welfare programs is shown in the adjoining charts. If the parties had maintained virtually identical welfare programs, there would have been a Rightist majority by 1962; the more generous Leftist program of the late '50s served to solidify and increase the Leftist majority.

## The Confirmation of Complex Theories

This is, admittedly, a rather freely constructed story, which is anchored at some points but not at others in statistical facts from 1954-55. Its gross prediction is fairly accurate. The actual division of the popular vote for the entire Swedish electorate, not just our age cohort, is shown in the following table:

|      | Per Cent | |
|------|---------------------|--------------------|
|      | Bourgeois Parties | Socialist Parties |
| 1952 | 49.6 | 50.4 |
| 1956 | 50.4 | 49.6 |
| 1958 | 50.4 | 49.6 |
| 1960 | 47.4 | 52.7 |

Source: *Statistisk Arsbok* 1962

Our allegory can be further used to reveal that even if the parties of the Right in 1962 change their mind—as has been done by some—and adopt the Socialist welfare plan, they will not gain a majority until the '70s, if present rates of mobility, differential fertility, and spread of the middle-class way of life prevail. This type of conclusion indicates a key feature of sociological simulations. They can estimate outcomes of alternative possibilities and give guidance in policy choice. And, once a simulation is established, one can keep it realistic by adjusting the rates of the variables involved and by adding new variables as they become relevant.

It would take us too far afield to discuss how simulations are done on an electronic computer. Suffice it to say that this way of formulating and testing theories can be done with ease and great speed on the standard models of electronic calculators that are now available.

Many persons can correctly predict an election, and the fact that a simulation gives a correct master prediction is no important confirmation of its truth. To test a simulation one makes many partial predictions which can be checked. In an election simulation these may be predictions of votes by sexes, by areas of the country, by different age groups. Only when a very high proportion—say, 90 to 95 per cent—of a large number of such partial predictions also prove accurate does one begin to trust the simulation. In reality, one achieves this degree of accuracy only by systematic tinkering with the variables.

82

## CONCLUDING REMARKS

Nothing in our discussion has indicated that it is impossible to obtain a sociological theory which is as well verified as theories are in other sciences. We can only express the hope that theorizing and verificational studies contributing to this end will attract attention from the sociologists of the future to the same extent that taxonomy and descriptive studies do.

If anything stands out from our review, it is the realization that there are great difficulties in testing a detached hypothesis compared to testing a hypothesis integrated into a theory. (See pp. 70-71 and 75-76). This has some important implications for the strategy of advancing sociological knowledge: verification is easier in studies suggested by sociological theory than in other studies.

Yet most problems for social research at present are not suggested by theoretical sociology. They are suggested by the whim or wisdom of foundation officials; by clients who want sociological help to acquire a larger share of markets, commodities or votes; by journalists, clergymen, and others who choose to debate certain issues of the day as social problems. The typical sociological research project is an *ad hoc* study of topics suggested by non-sociologists. It is a sheer accident when these topics can be integrated in sociological theory. The studies of these top-

83

ics, accordingly, face difficult problems of verification. Moreover, they are not cumulative; the best that can be said for them is that they foster methodological advances.

By contrast, the studies suggested by existing theory are cumulative, and their problems of verification are modest. This state of affairs, when a theory guides the choice of research topics, is "normal science", and it prevails until the research findings no longer seem in regular agreement with the postulates of the theory and alternatives are formulated. At such a point, it no longer suffices merely to amend and elaborate the theory; the scientific community goes through a "revolution" and the Young Turks emerge with a novel theory, which serves as a guide to novel research topics.[1] Such has been the historical pattern of most sciences, and we would be bad sociologists to assume that our science would progress differently.

Thus the next task for sociology would be to continue with great dedication to sum up its knowledge in the form of theory and to use this theory to gain control over its research efforts.

LIVERPOOL
UNIVERSITY

---

[1] Thomas Kuhn, *The Structure of Scientific Revolutions*, (Chicago: University of Chicago Press, 1962). It might be noted that "normal science" serves the needs of practitioners more through applied theory than applied research.